Teaching Refugee Children

www.teachingrefugeechildren.com

© 2018, Hélène van Oudheusden
Cover drawing: Sophia Mariola
ISBN 9789081440011

All rights reserved. No part of this book may be used or reproduced in any manner whatsoever without written permission of Hélène van Oudheusden, Apollo Books. For information: info@helenevanoudheusden.nl

By the same author:
Connecting Values, Multicultural Guidance for Primary Education
(available in Dutch only)

Hélène van Oudheusden

TEACHING REFUGEE CHILDREN

A Hero's Journey

Apollo Books

For Habiba

*Your courage and radiance
are pure empowerment*

I met Habiba during my voluntary work. She is 11 years old and has been waiting in a refugee camp for two years. Habiba wants to go to school but there are no teachers. She taught herself six languages to make the most of her waiting time.

REVIEWS

Teaching Refugee Children is awesome. What a wonderful tool for helping these children! | Joseph Campbell Foundation, USA

Education and guidance of refugee children can be surprisingly clear and fruitful. Van Oudheusden has the talent to make this big and often overwhelming issue approachable, having achieved an equilibrium between the empathic and the practical. | Teacher at the Royal Academy of Arts, The Hague, The Netherlands

I would like to highly recommend Teaching Refugee Children to all people who deal with refugee children, either as teachers or as caregivers. This book even helps us, parents, to maintain a loving understanding relationship with our children and with ourselves! | Counsellor on Lesvos, Greece

[..] At least as important in the book of Hélène is the attention for the professional/volunteer who works with refugees: this work can only be done well, with perseverence, if you take good care of yourself and when you take time to reflect on your own well-being.. Because only then can you bring the pleasure and compassion into your work that these children need so much. An indispensable book for everyone who works with refugees! | Practitioner refugee reception, the Hague, the Netherlands

In these multicultural times this book is the next step for more empathy for refugee children. Teaching Refugee Children supports you to reflect on the teachers who give the children hope in the future through education. A very valuable book! | Marie-Cecile van den Boom, Belgium

I have read this book with admiration for the writer. The book shows empathy for not only people who work with refugee children but for everyone who has to do with work, family, relationships or with inner work. All is described very clearly and well supported with the model of Joseph Campbell, the Hero's Journey. I highly recommend this book as a self-help book for everyone! | Teacher, the Netherlands

In her book Teaching Refugee Children, Hélène van Oudheusden uses the Hero's Journey (Joseph Campbell) succesfully. In this practical manual she guides teachers step by step to their inner world where one becomes aware of one's own feelings and perceptions. With exercises and many tips, the teacher learns to turn these skills into an effective lesson plan adapted to the experiences and feelings of refugee children. | Teacher, Switzerland

[..] In addition to the practical content, Teaching Refugee Children is touching and pleasantly readable. Teaching Refugee Children invites me to get started right away! | Teacher, the Netherlands

One of the eye-openers for me is the importance of knowing about the cultural background of each child. I highly recommend Teaching Refugee Children to every teacher who has the privilege of educating refugee children! | Volunteer unaccompanied minors, Lesvos, Greece

Teaching Refugee Children is an energizing book for teachers. It is written in simple English and perfectly applicable in the classroom. This book serves as a daily reminder for compassionate teaching. | Shannon Molkenboer, the Netherlands

INHOUD

Acknowledgments	11
Foreword	13

PART 1

1. Self-care when teaching refugee children	17
1.1 Introduction	17
1.2 First take care of yourself, teacher	18
1.3 Energy flows where attention goes	26
1.4 Self-reflection when teaching refugee children	27
1.5 Keeping up to date	32

PART 2

2. Care of refugee children	37
2.1 Introduction	37
2.2 Social-emotional learning (SEL)	37
2.3 Maslow pyramid – the hierarchy of human needs	38
2.4 Which psychological effects refugee children are facing?	39
2.5 Effects of trauma in the classroom	43

PART 3

3. Trauma-sensitive teaching	46
3.1 Introduction	46
3.2 The Power of Community	47
3.3 Phases in creating a class community	48
3.4 Say Hello - Say Goodbye Exercises – Rites of Passage	51
3.5 Tools for trauma-sensitive teaching	53
3.6 Special attention for unaccompanied minors	67
3.7 Summary of do's for powerful guidance of refugee children	68
3.8 What we sometimes do not think about...	70

PART 4
4. The Hero's Journey – Rites of Passage ... 73

PART 5
5. Refugee children advising teachers ... 100

PART 6
6. Refugee teachers advising teachers ... 104

PART 7
7. Universal values in practice ... 108
7.1 Introduction ... 108
7.2 Connection ... 108
7.3 Trust ... 113
7.4 Compassion ... 116
7.5 Exercises for teachers only ... 118
7.6 Do's for school directors ... 121

PART 8
8. Mindfulness for Refugee Children ... 124
8.1 Introduction ... 124
8.2 Advantages of mindfulness ... 125
8.3 When do you use mindfulness exercises? ... 125
8.4 Breathe in, breathe out ... 126
8.5 One minute mindfulness ... 126
8.6 Five to ten minutes mindfulness ... 127
8.7 Ten minutes mindfulness ... 136

Inspirational reading and watching ... 138
Sources ... 141
Extra for readers ... 145
About the author ... 146

ACKNOWLEDGMENTS

When I saw the many dinghies with refugee children arriving on Greek shores I could not believe my eyes. There is a strange physical and emotional reaction when you witness boat landings. The adrenaline rush is sky high because you never know whether all people on board are safe. You don't even know whether to laugh or cry. The cries of children and their parents will stay in my heart forever. Cries of joy and of sorrow. For having left their homes and loved ones behind, for their relief about a (mostly) safe landing, trusting that a new life could begin by entering Europe. For every refugee child I met and for every child that tries his best to adapt to a new life in a strange country I wished to write this book. Thank you for allowing me into your world…

The writing process was a truly joint-effort. I could not have done this without the support, inspiration and love of many people. We are truly all part of a long chain of helpers along the route refugee children are taking.

With my deep gratitude for your contribution to this book I would like to thank: **Petra Martina Reichmann, Michael Lambert, Joseph Campbell Foundation, Cees van Oudheusden, Joke van Oudheusden, Hanneke Steenbergen-Geurtz, Sophia Mariola, Esther Kraaijenbrink, Sharda Jainandunsing, Jay Riem Vis, Dionisis Pavlou and all dedicated teachers for your willingness to share your experience and ideas on educating refugee children with colleagues from all over the world!**

FOREWORD

"This isn't work, it's my passion. I feel so grateful that I am allowed to teach refugee children."

This is what refugee teachers tell me, time and again. The stamina of refugee teachers and their dedication to their pupils constantly amazes me. No matter where a refugee teacher is based I notice the same love for children and the same thankfulness for their job. When you love your job this much there is always the possibility that you might overlook to take care of yourself as a person and a teacher. Therefore this book starts with a self-care chapter to support you daily.

Currently there are over 20 million displaced children worldwide (UNHCR). To empower refugee children in their daily challenging lives it is important to help them develop sustainable self-worth, self-confidence and persistence. This social-emotional learning (SEL) is the foundation for a successful education in refugee communities and in schools. This way a child can view her future from inner strength and see all the possibilities available to her.

Teaching Refugee Children offers you theory, tools and exercises to support yourself and your pupils in social-emotional learning. We will look at the education and guidance of refugee children from a psychological and spiritual point of view. It is the perspective of transforming your life to be reborn into a new life. The important work of Joseph Campbell, mythologist and author of The Hero with a Thousand Faces was one of the inspirations for this book. The Hero's Journey describes the inner (and in the case of refugees outer) journey of life. The schema is adapted to the lives of refugee children and their teachers, to support you to guide the child in his personal hero's journey.

Since 2006 I have provided social-emotional learning for refugee children in the Netherlands. We have welcomed children from over 125 countries into schools. Each with their own story, needs, wishes and dreams for the future. In my first book, Connecting Values, Multicultural Guidance for Primary Education, I described how the use of universal values helps you to create harmony for (refugee) children in multicultural schools. In 2015/2016 I volunteered on Lesvos, Greece, during the influx of 750.000 (mainly) Syrian and Afghan refugees. I am still touched by this opportunity to witness the plight of refugee children during their journey. Following I have organised international study visits to Lesvos to educate teachers in trauma-sensitive teaching.

Connecting Values was written for children already living in their new homeland. During my field work in the Netherlands and in Greece I meet dedicated, inspiring (refugee) teachers doing the best they can in challenging circumstances. This inspired me to write a book especially for the numerous teachers educating migrant and refugee children all over the world. Teaching Refugee Children is a practical manual that supports you to trauma-sensitively fill the gap between the lack of (years of) education and the day the children start thriving again in their new school. Whether you are a volunteer teacher in a makeshift school or are educating refugee children in their new homeland, this book is for you. Its aim is to support you in your important work: raising a new generation.

Hélène van Oudheusden

Note, in the context of this book 'child' is used to mean children up to 18 years of age.

TIP | Visit www.teachingrefugeechildren.com for extra tools, exercises and all weblinks in this book.

PART 1

"...The teacher who walks in the shadow of the temple, among his followers, gives not of his wisdom but rather of his faith and his lovingness. If he is indeed wise he does not bid you to enter the house of his wisdom but rather leads you to the threshold of your own mind..."

Kahlil Gibran, The Prophet

TAGS

self-care | recharge your batteries | positive teaching self-reflection | burnout | Me Time | personal motivation international treaties

1 | SELF-CARE WHEN TEACHING REFUGEE CHILDREN

1.1 INTRODUCTION

Working with refugee children can take its toll on your teaching skills as well as your personal life. The stories of the children can sometimes be hard to bear, especially when it is challenging for you to manage the contrast of your privileged life with the hardships of the children and parents that you are supporting on a daily basis. Regularly teachers need to take time off work to heal themselves because they have spent too much of their empathy on their pupils, forgetting to take care of themselves along the way. You cannot pour from an empty cup!

Compassion and empathy are much needed virtues in life. However, it is always best to share compassion rather than giving it away. When sharing you are advised to be compassionate and kind to yourself first. Just as on a plane when you must first put the oxygen mask on yourself and then on your child.

self-care   In this chapter self-care is explored on different levels, enabling you to enhance your well-being through self-reflection and by implementing practical tools.

> **TIP** | *Everything that applies to regular education, also applies to educating refugee children. You just need to add even more warmth and compassion. Your pedagogical approach is more important than didactics in educating refugee children.*

1.2 FIRST TAKE CARE OF YOURSELF, TEACHER

"Know thyself"
Γνῶθι σεαυτόν
Temple of Apollo in Delphi, Greece

As a teacher of refugee children you will be confronted with the psychological and social effects of having fled and of having endured what can be a very difficult journey. Although you are not a psychologist and – as you are probably aware – should refer children for psychological counselling, it is helpful to know about the kind of psychological impacts fleeing from one's home country can have on children and their parents. Understanding this background can support you to understand the sometimes unexpected behaviours of children. Connection, trust and compassion are what a child needs from you at every stage. In Chapter 2 you will find information about psychological effects.

In order to share your values of connection, trust and compassion you need to apply these values to your own life as well. It is much easier to share qualities with others if you have enough to share! If you only give away connection, trust and compassion who is going to take care of you? Giving away means that you do not have it for yourself any more. Sharing means that you enjoy these qualities for yourself as well as for your pupils. Chapter 7 provides exercises on connection, trust and compassion.

Recharge your batteries

Self-care is crucial in educating refugee children. You can be confronted with personal stories that can be hard to grasp or process. It might be challenging for you to keep your personal and your working life separate. Especially when volunteering, teachers can be inclined to be 110% committed to their pupils. As volunteering work shows: it is most healthy for everyone involved if you use a relay system. It is vital to take leisure time away from the premises where you volunteer or work. It is also important to enjoy your time away without feeling guilty about having a steady place to live and a more secure living environment than the refugee children you work with.

recharge your batteries Please take time to recharge your own batteries. It is not possible to pour from an empty cup and only you can fill your own cup!

1. How do you recharge your energy?

_____
_____
_____
_____

2. Who will fill in for you when you are sick?

_____
_____
_____
_____

3. How do you ask for what you want? Do you hold back because you think your wishes and needs will not be met? Remember that people cannot read your mind, only when we ask for what we need can others know how to help us.

_____
_____
_____
_____

5 Tools for recharging

1. **Debrief** with your colleagues every day. It is vital to talk through what you have experienced and to be able to go home and lead 'your other life'.
2. **Stay in touch** with your friends and family back home via calling, visiting, WhatsApp and social media.
3. **Take your ideas seriously**, you are the expert on teaching refugee children. Write down any ideas you might have and share them with people who could make them happen.
4. **If bureaucracy is holding you back** in the organisation you are working with, look around you for grass roots organisations that might be in need of your expertise.
5. **Eat healthily, get enough sleep and be sure to exercise!** Your pupils learn more from what you do than from what you say. You are their role model.

Positive teaching

While educating refugee children you are constantly challenged by looking at what cán be done. You may have to deal with insufficient financial resources, the unexpected arrival and departure of pupils, lack of protocol and a lack of clarity about what a child has experienced on their journey. These are all challenges you need to handle while teaching.

Do not be discouraged. Keep up the positive teaching ánd thinking. If your starting point is 'What can be done in this situation?' you will create space and possibilities for yourself. You don't need to be perfect or to teach perfectly, often 'good' is 'good enough'.

positive teaching

Self-care when teaching refugee children

An appointment with yourself is also an appointment

self-appointment

Working hard, making that one last phone call, reluctantly participating in yet another working group, asking for extra funds or thinking about your own fundraising campaigns via social media. Challenges and temptations are part of daily life in schools. For children and also for teachers. We are teaching children to take care of themselves, to set their own boundaries and to engage with each other socially.

And what about you?

self-reflection

1. How well are you taking care of yourself, physically, emotionally, mentally and spiritually?

_____
_____
_____
_____

self-care

2. Are you clear about your own boundaries and how do you communicate them to others?

_____
_____
_____
_____

3. What inspires you most in your contact with colleagues?

_____
_____
_____

4. When do you have enough space for your personal growth?

_____
_____
_____
_____

5. Is self-care regularly on the agenda of (staff) meetings?

_____
_____
_____
_____

6. What does your soul need to recharge?

_____
_____
_____
_____

7. How many self-care appointments did you make with yourself this week?

_____
_____
_____
_____

Prevent teacher burnout

Self-care is of growing interest in schools. There is an important reason for this: worldwide the rate of teacher burnout - where teachers experience feelings of physical, emotional and mental exhaustion - is very high. As Jenny Grant Rankin Ph.D. wrote in 'The Teacher Burnout Epidemic, Part 1 of 2':

"There is a steady supply of research on teacher burnout coming from Africa, Asia, Australia, Canada, Europe, the Middle East, New Zealand, and South America. For example, nearly half of teachers in India suffer from burnout (Shukla & Trivedi, 2008) and half of male and female teachers studied in southern Jordan suffer from emotional exhaustion associated with burnout."

Alkhateeb, Kraishan, & Salah, 2015 (Psychology Magazine)

teachingrefugeechildren.com for all weblinks

In the Netherlands 1 in 5 educational workers experience a burnout, according to Statistics Netherlands.

The reasons for burnout vary but are often caused by a combination of factors including intense emotional involvement with the job, ever increasing administrative responsibilities, a lack of support from colleagues/management/parents and difficulties in class management. Class management is sometimes influenced by the challenging home situations of the children, especially when there is domestic violence, poverty, drug or alcohol abuse.

TIP | *As for refugee teachers: you cannot stop the war, poverty or discrimination... So please take care of your boundaries.*

As a general rule, you could say that when burnout symptoms arise teachers have used more energy than they had to give. They have been unable to re-charge and their batteries are flat. How do you recharge during the day or after work? Do you ever switch off your phone? Do you and your colleagues send messages in the evenings? Are you trying to catch up with work in front of the television with your laptop? That is not recharging, that is prolonging your working day…

phone in flight mode while sleeping to avoid radiation – yes, your alarm clock will still work

Having Me Time is essential

When was the last time you made an appointment with yourself? You don't need to say that you are not available for a meeting tomorrow at 16.00 o'clock because you have a date with yourself. Block your personal time and be loyal to that. There is nothing noble about continuously ignoring your body and the inner signals that say that you are tired. Nor in losing your pleasure in doing your work just because you want to try to avoid your colleagues thinking you are being selfish. That will not happen easily and you will set your colleagues and the children you teach a beautiful example by taking care of your boundaries. This is a sustainable investment in your own well-being as well as in the education of the new generation that has been entrusted to you.

me-time

Are you tired of school work and thinking about working less?
First check if you can do less work for school at home.
That might give you more energy immediately.
This comment of her husband helped a primary school teacher look at her workload with fresh eyes.

You must recharge yourself, especially during busy periods - by the way, it seems to be 'just a busy period' at every school every week of the school year! So, how can you recharge?

7 Extra tips to:
- Do your work with more energy and inspiration
- Have more grip on your work and on the pedagogical climate
- Deal more smoothly with unexpected changes during the day

1. **Be critical** about which meetings you attend.
2. **Meet standing,** then 30 minutes are often sufficient to consult effectively. Is more time needed? Then split up into groups and come back an hour later to present your action items.
3. Try to **pay attention to what you offer** in meetings: is your input to the point or do you sometimes want to say something only to show that you are present? Do not repeat what somebody else already said. This saves a lot of time you could use in other ways. Do you have the courage to attend a meeting and to speak only when it is relevant, new and to the point?
4. **Vary your route to school**, preferably through nature. Cycle if that is possible.
5. **Your manager is also a human being.** He or she may want to drink coffee first when they arrive at school - instead of having to answer all sorts of questions as soon as they get through the door.
6. **You do not need to be active in WhatsApp groups** if you do not want to be, turn off the notifications and check your messages once a day.
7. Are you often disturbed by children from other classes or colleagues entering your classroom? **Stick a kind, friendly 'Please do not disturb' notice on your classroom door** and do not send your pupils around to other classes (too early) for treats. As a colleague said: "Since I started to respect my colleagues' classes more and not disturb them, I've noticed that colleagues do not enter my classes unexpectedly anymore either."

1.3 ENERGY FLOWS WHERE ATTENTION GOES

Sometimes we are so consumed by the pressure in our work that we forget why we once chose to become a refugee teacher. The following questions help you to recover your personal motivation. *personal motivation* Working from your original motivation supports you to balance what you give and receive in teaching.

Checklist questions

1. Which situation or person inspired you to become a teacher?

_____

_____

_____

_____

2. How do you take responsibility for the way you function at school?

_____

_____

_____

_____

3. In what way is self-reflection part of your self-care?

_____

_____

_____

_____

1.4 SELF-REFLECTION WHEN TEACHING REFUGEE CHILDREN

This worksheet was first published in my book 'Connecting Values, Multicultural Guidance for Primary Education' (2010) and has been adapted for this book.

self-research

Please be aware that (sub)conscious thoughts and beliefs influence your work as a teacher. Changing thoughts and personal opinions will change your reality since energy flows where attention goes. You can use the questions below for self-research into your (sub)conscious motives for teaching refugee children.

1. What thoughts or opinions do you have about the current multicultural society? Which aspects appeal to you most and which appeal to you less?

_____
_____
_____
_____

2. How do you feel about the arrival of refugees in your homeland?

_____
_____
_____
_____

3. Did you make a conscious choice to teach at a school for refugee children or at a multicultural school? If so, why?

_____
_____
_____
_____

4. Which of your ideas and expectations about working with pupils from other cultures and countries have proven true and which ones haven't (yet)?

_____
_____
_____
_____

5. How do you feel about your colleagues and supervisors? About your pupils' parents?

_____
_____
_____
_____

6. How do you think they feel about you?

_____
_____
_____

7. Do you have the impression that you sometimes unconsciously show your thoughts or assumptions about others through body language?

_____
_____
_____
_____

8. Have you ever talked about your thoughts and ideas with others to see if they are correct?

_____
_____
_____
_____

9. What is the greatest gift for you in your work with children from other cultures?

_____
_____
_____
_____

disappointment

10. What, if anything, disappoints you in your job?

_____
_____
_____

11. If you did not consciously opt for your current job - for example because the school population has changed during your time working there - do you like your job? Which aspects of your job do you like more or less? What are you doing to keep your job fulfilling?

_____
_____
_____
_____

12. Are these aspects directly related to working in a multicultural school or are they separate from the school composition?

_____
_____
_____
_____

13. Do you find it fascinating to deal with pupils from different countries of origin and their parents? Which are the easiest things to do and what is difficult for you?

_____
_____
_____
_____

14. If you needed extra support in guiding (one or more) pupils with language deficits, would you ask for that support? Who would you ask?

_____

_____

_____

headscarf

15. Are you willing to take into account varying cultural habits in your lessons? It is known that girls who wear a headscarf can hear a little less as a result of their ears being covered. Would you be able or willing to make extra effort to involve those pupils in the lesson?

_____

_____

_____

_____

Result

satisfaction

You have the tools to take responsibility for your well-being at school and therefore improve the pedagogical climate in your lessons. You can prepare your lessons and your classroom in such a way that you achieve the results you have in mind. Such as pupils who participate attentively in lessons and a feeling of satisfaction at the end of your working day.

1.5 KEEPING UP TO DATE WITH EDUCATIONAL AND HUMAN RIGHTS DEVELOPMENTS

In times of stress (and most days in refugee schools or communities contain underlying feelings of anxiety, insecurity and pressure) you can lose sight of the importance of reading interesting articles and books or watching videos on teaching (refugee children).

When was the last time you:
- Read a vocational magazine?
- Truly talked with a colleague about education in order to improve your lessons?
- Attended a seminar on educating newcomers?

If you have a communication system with parents, inform them about your recent vocational schooling. They like to hear about this because it enhances their trust in you as the main formal educator of their child. Sharing and communicating with parents may lead to interesting conversations and new perspectives, therefore (even) more commitment/participation in school. And... actively involved parents increase the feelings of safety a child has in their school career. The child may feel its parents' support as a warm blanket. *parental participation*

How international treaties affect your pupils

- Do you know the universal rights of the child (convention on the rights of the child (CRC)?
- What is the essence of the Dublin Regulation?
- Are you aware of the EU-Turkey Statement & Action Plan?

international treaties

One, two or all three of these are important in the (daily) life of the children in your class. Inform yourself about the main points from these statements. This knowledge helps you to better understand the psychology and some of the behaviours of children.

It is not about knowing the specifics of all the international treaties, but if you are aware of their essence it can help you to better understand news and to see the behaviour of children and parents in a broader perspective. This can lead to inspiring communication and connection between teachers and pupils.

EXAMPLE | *Under the EU-Turkey deal, refugees arriving after 20 March 2016 on the Greek islands (Europe) can be returned to Turkey after their asylum procedure. What if a refugee family has already been granted asylum in Europe but the mother has been waiting in Greece for a family reunification since June 2016? Can she travel? Will she be returned to Turkey? The tensions that this situation can cause in a family could affect the behaviour of the children in the classroom.*

TIP | *Talking with parents about the seminar you attended on multicultural competences can improve communication between the parents of children in your classroom.*

NOTES

Care of refugee children

PART 2

أنت جميلة كما أنت

You are beautiful just the way you are

TAGS

social-emotional learning (SEL) | the Hero's Journey
Maslow | psychological effects | trauma in the classroom

2 | CARE OF REFUGEE CHILDREN

2.1 INTRODUCTION

65.6 million refugees experience intense transformations

Worldwide 65.6 million people are on the move, fleeing from war, oppression, poverty and climate change. 22.5 million of them are children. They are growing up in refugee camps or in a new country. Every day about 28.300 people are forced to flee from their homes because of war or persecution. Many of these 'numbers' are children and all are people. Each with his or her own story, history, hopes and dreams. Every child has the right to tailor-made guidance when processing his experiences and rebuilding his life.

UNHCR, Figures at a Glance (weblink at Sources)

'numbers' are children

2.2 SOCIAL-EMOTIONAL LEARNING (SEL)

It is in the best interests of the child, their parents, the school and society that children are able to integrate well. This also applies to refugee children in camps where social-emotional learning (SEL) has to be part of the daily routine. Even when it is not yet possible to offer an elaborate school curriculum, it is crucial to work with SEL-tools such as the core values of connection, trust and compassion. A child who learns to connect with themselves and with others builds trust in their self and others and can grow up to be a conscious, happy world citizen with compassion for both themselves and the world around them. All tools in this book are focused on improving social-emotional learning.

social-emotional learning (SEL)

universal values

Every soul has its unique purpose in life. The challenges for refugee children are huge… The experience of being uprooted, of having had to leave everything you know, love and care about behind to start a new life in an unfamiliar place has a deep impact on the souls of refugees and their children.

soul purpose

The main metaphor for the inner and outward journey of the soul used in this book is the Hero's Journey (Joseph Campbell). This psychological model describes the inner transformations one experiences when going through a (big) change in life. The model is applied to both refugee teachers and refugee children (Chapter 4).

the Hero's Journey

> Arriving in another climate, meeting hostile people and having to learn a new alphabet can be scary for children.

2.3 MASLOW PYRAMID – THE HIERARCHY OF HUMAN NEEDS

The experiences of refugee children – of being uprooted, having had to leave everything they knew and loved behind to start a new life in an unknown place - have a deep impact on their hearts and souls. The Maslow pyramid explains the hierarchy of human needs. First and foremost, safety and security in basic matters is needed, then comes the need to belong to a community. Once those needs are met there is room for self-development. For refugee children who were deprived of food and safety for a long time, it can take a lot of dedication before they are able to open up to wishing to be part of a community again. When they feel this social safety they can – at their own pace – start being an active participant in, for example, Life Skills Classes (see Chapter 3.5).

Maslow pyramid

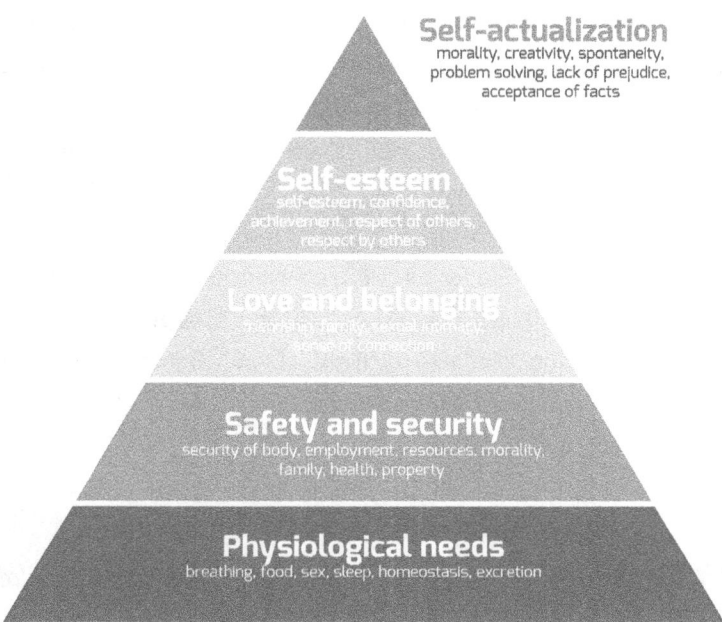

2.4 WHICH PSYCHOLOGICAL EFFECTS REFUGEE CHILDREN ARE FACING?

Refugee children and their parents have experienced immense challenges when it comes to basic safety and security in their lives. Children have no influence over the choice their parents made to flee. They are also not the cause of war or economic scarcity in their country of origin. However, because children are so open to influences around them, they suffer the most from the flight. Afterwards they have to go on no matter what has happened to them. They must also process their emotions and feelings about ordeals that most other people will probably never experience and/or would get professional help with.

psychological effects   Once refugee families arrive in their new or temporary homeland they might start to feel more secure. However, be aware that when routine returns in their lives there is a change from being in survivor mode to dealing with the normal day to day life. This can cause new challenges such as a continuance of the survivor mode where it is no longer needed. Will I still be robbed, am I safe or can I get sexually assaulted here, who can I trust?

Problems can continue for a while, even when a family seems to be able to start building a new life. It will often take several years to slowly process and eliminate the flight – fright – fight reactions that they needed to rely on for a long time.

YARO | *9 Year old Yaro travelled from South Sudan through Africa to Lebanon. He and his family of four walked and got lifts from people (hitchhiked). They were travelling for five months. What did Yaro experience on the following levels:*

1. Physical – his bodily experiences | *It was extremely cold at night and the roads were unsafe. Many days there was not enough food. He couldn't wash his clothes for weeks.*

2. Emotional – his feelings | *Some people he met on the way were kind to children, many were not.*

3. Mental – his thoughts, ideas, concepts | *Yaro was confused by the unreliability of people. He could never figure out what someone's true intentions were.*

4. Spiritual – what his soul experienced | *As young as he was, Yaro already worried about life's questions. He wondered what the meaning of his life was when he encountered so much hostility from people while he had done nothing wrong.*

Scientific research shows that refugee children have to deal with many complex psychological and physical effects. Professor of Child Psychiatry Panos Vostanis mentions the following effects in 'How to help refugee children get through the trauma of what's happened to them':

- Post-traumatic stress
- Depression and anxiety
- Physical ill health
- Developmental delays
- Social exclusion
- Lack of education

He adds: "Refugee children are very vulnerable to extreme poverty, exploitation, abuse, neglect and parental mental illness. They can also struggle to adjust to their host country or environment. These risks are even more pronounced for unaccompanied minors and former child soldiers."

Psychological and emotional support for refugee children is therefore the first priority. You, as a teacher, could be one of the first caretakers a refugee child meets. You will find tools for trauma-sensitive teaching to support the well-being of the child in Part 3.

social care network Ideally a strong social care network should be available for your pupils where they receive:
1. Professional support to process their trauma(s).
2. Coping mechanisms to handle their trauma(s).

family life 3. Social-emotional guidance to regain trust in people.
4. Possibilities to discover that despite the circumstances they can still be happy.

Doctors without Borders in 'Reshaping the Trauma of Refugee Children in Lesvos', National Geographic. Weblink in Sources.

Unfortunately this is not always the case. If there is limited social care available the UNHCR provides exercises for teachers in their manual 'Teaching About Refugees – Guidance on working with refugee children struggling with stress and trauma'. A weblink to this manual can be found in the Sources section at the end of this book.

trauma in classroom

> It is remarkable to see the strength, resilience, hope and persistence in refugee children.

Learning a new language

Some studies show that learning a new language helps refugee children to integrate. However, other studies show that learning a new language can also disrupt family life since the child's level of language education is often (temporarily) higher than that of their parents. When a child learns the language of the new homeland, they can become the interpreter for the family and therefore be burdened by paperwork and bureaucracy as well as being involved in conversations that are too complicated for their age. Because of this the child loses their childhood twice: the first time because of war and the second time because they are burdened with adult tasks.
http://www.vocativ.com/news/230358/wont-someone-think-of-the-children/index.html

2.5 EFFECTS OF TRAUMA IN THE CLASSROOM

The following table shows how the effects of trauma can be expressed by children in the classroom and what you can do to help them. It is advised to refer children to a mental health professional when you have concerns.

Trauma	Effect in class	Required
1. Fled from a (perhaps always unsafe) homeland	Fear of unexpected sounds	Remain calm and be predictable
2. Having lived temporarily in different places/ countries	Confusion about structure	Clear structure and continued connection
3. War, terror or experiences of torture (of family members)	Grief, anxiety, having missed role models	If needed: mental health practitioner
4. Hunger, cold, lack of hygiene during the flight.	Slower brain development	Compassion, understanding and patience
5. People smugglers who (can) use violence	Difficulty trusting adults	Predictability and be trustworthy
6. Lack of education and relaxation	Lower self-esteem because of new language and difficulty adapting to structure	Patience and calmness
7. Fear of dying themselves or fear that parents might die	Lack of trust	Compassion
8. Encounters with unknown cultures, languages and people	Either flexibility and / or mistrust	Patience

© Hélène van Oudheusden

How the brain is affected

brain A child's brain can be overwhelmed by unprocessed intense experiences. This can cause confusion in the mind at unexpected moments. The reptile, instinctive hindbrain (at the back of the head) is where emotions are stored. The frontal lobes handle the processing of information and conscious thinking. When emotions have not yet been worked through, such as in cases of stress and trauma, the reptile brain can be over alert and the thinking brain cannot keep up. This is when impulsive physical or emotional behaviour is most likely to occur.

On trust and 'not being here'

Refugee children need additional guidance to be able to deal with these effects and also to (learn to) trust their bodily signals again, or to trust adults (for example a teacher) again. Only when a child feels comfortable can they open up to learning. Just imagine: how well are you be able to focus when a painful private situation is occupying your mind? These things are very distracting. For children - who have fewer tools to deal with their thoughts and feelings than adults do – it is an almost impossible task. Having the space to be able to just sit and look out of the window might help the child. Seeing trees can have a relaxing effect. It is not that they are not paying attention, they are feeding themselves with energy from nature.

You may notice that some pupils seem to be 'not totally present' at certain moments. Their minds can wander to previous experiences, a staring child may therefore well be processing emotions and feelings. It is too difficult for him or her to focus on the lesson at the same time. Knowing this might help you as a teacher to let the child 'be' and to just keep an eye on him. Please refer the child to a mental health specialist.

In the absence of appropriate, qualified support the UNHCR manual 'How to deal with memory flashbacks and episodes where students appear 'not there'?' may be of use. Although I have a different approach this manual is a valuable resource for unsupported teachers.

Trauma-sensitive teaching

PART·3

"A true community begins in the hearts of the people involved. It is not a place of distraction but a place of being."

Malidoma Patrice Somé,
Ritual: Power, Healing and Community

TAGS

trauma-sensitive teaching | creating a class community | rituals | emotional scripting | Say Hello – Say Goodbye | 6 senses | mindfulness exercises

3 | TRAUMA-SENSITIVE TEACHING = A WARM PEDAGOGICAL CLIMATE FOR NEWCOMERS

3.1 INTRODUCTION

Warmth is the key to teaching refugee children. Creating a safe blanket around the classroom supports children to heal from their experiences and to gradually start to thrive again.

As the UNHCR states: "Whilst some refugee children can present challenging and worrying behavior at school and in the classroom, not all children who have experienced armed conflict and flight will suffer from trauma and stress."

Teaching About Refugees, Guidance on working with refugee children struggling with stress and trauma. A weblink to this manual can be found in the Sources section at the end of this book.

Whether a refugee child is traumatised or not can only be assessed by a healthcare professional. It is advised to refer children to a mental health practitioner if you have concerns about their mental health. Teaching in a trauma-sensitive way is nurturing for all children. It does not require a different didactic approach but rather is a deepening of how you already prefer to teach children: with understanding, softness and by offering safety and structure. If you can ensure that the child feels safe again, the child can restore their self-regulation. This knowledge can help teachers to look at the child's intentions rather than to focus on unexpected behaviour. Compassion will help smooth contact with the child.

trauma-sensitive teaching

In this chapter you will explore the power of creating a strong community for the children in your care. This includes practical exercises for arriving and departing pupils. The tools for trauma-sensitive teaching are applicable on every school day and the schema with do's for powerful guidance of children completes this chapter.

3.2 THE POWER OF COMMUNITY

Being part of a community is something everybody needs in life. Feeling at home, surrounding yourself with likeminded friends or colleagues and having a safe base from which to explore the world is a basic human need. School is the perfect place for children to feel connected with classmates and teachers. A stable community helps the child to process their experiences and to make new friends. Forming a community is not always easy but working with core values addresses the inner need people have to give and receive respect, gratitude, co-operation, connection, trust and compassion. Making it easier to form a community based on these values.

class community

We are all family

When teaching refugee children from different cultural backgrounds you may also experience tension between children. This can be hard, especially if the children speak amongst themselves in their own language and you cannot understand what is going on. Or, if you are not aware of the roots of historical (cultural) differences. Solving differences and fights is part of social-emotional learning. Sometimes teachers try to solve tensions between pupils by explaining that we are all different people, each with their own talents. An experienced refugee teacher noticed that this approach did not work in her class one year. When she changed her intervention from 'We are all different' to 'We are all family' she noticed that children responded calmly and with understanding. Being family was their value for

we are family

creating a warm community together. Just like in any group (in schools, amongst friends, in companies etc.) there is a series of dynamics group members have to go through before they can form a fully functioning (performing) group where everybody feels at home. These phases are explained in the next paragraph.

> **TIP** | *When faced with continuing fights in class that seem to be related to cultural differences it can be helpful to explain to the children that 'We are all family'. This approach focuses on the talents, thoughts and emotions we share instead of arguing about differences.*

3.3 PHASES IN CREATING A CLASS COMMUNITY

Psychologist Bruce Tuckman created the group dynamics model of 'forming, storming, norming, performing and adjourning/mourning' to explain the stages every group passes through on its way to (high) performance. In a group where children are arriving and leaving all the time this model may operate under pressure cooker like conditions. Positions within the group, who is a leader, who a follower, what the norms and official rules are, become extra challenges for both teacher and children. Each stage has its own characteristics.

creating a class community

Forming

In this first phase children can be anxious and/or waiting. They are getting to know each other and the new teacher. The children are looking for guidance and safety because they do not know the rules yet.

influence the stages of group dynamics

Teacher

- Provide structure and predictability (Chapter 3.5)
- Create special focus to include everybody in the group
- Offer group dynamics games such as Freeze - pupils walk around until the teacher says Freeze! They hold their position until the teachers tells them to move again.

Storming

The children are starting to test boundaries. They may understand what the rules are but wish to express their individuality. They perceive themselves as individuals and not yet as group members. You may experience more friction between children as they are trying to find their way. Or children may also challenge your leadership.

Teacher

- Express your leadership clearly
- Explain this model to the children to help them understand that this phase will pass
- Let the children co-create the class rules

Norming

Gradually children will express their need for shared rules and ways of communicating. How do we wish to be as a group? What can we offer each other (instead of protecting only our own interests)? They start respecting each other and accepting the teacher as their authority.

Teacher

- Introduce socialising games such as The Web of All Together (Chapter 3.4)
- Make sure every child is heard
- Evaluate class dynamics with the children daily to inspire their sense of community

- Offer lessons about universal values and norms.
   Formulate class rules in a positive way.
   No: we don't run inside the school
   Yes: we walk inside the school

> *Be aware that your class may regress to a previous stage at any time because of the introduction of new topics to your curriculum or because of the arrival or departure of children. Every change is likely to lead to another set of dynamics - your insight into these phases may help you understand and deal with this more easily.*

Performing

Everything is clear to everyone involved. The program, the sense of community, the way we help each other in class. There will be less fighting and bullying. Children start taking more initiative and responsibility for their education. New arrivals or children leaving will not have a huge impact on the performing stage. Now you can enjoy that you and your class have reached the performing stage.

Teacher
- Don't relax too much! The children still need to feel you are the leader
- Take extra time to support individual children

Adjourning/mourning

The group enters this last phase at the end of the school year or when a larger number of children arrive or leave. You may notice that children experience more fights or irritations. This could be because saying goodbye can be easier when you are angry with someone… That way you don't have to feel sad about maybe never meeting again. It is crucial to say goodbye in a comforting and loving way. To honour the group that you made together and that gave you special experiences.

Teacher

goodbye exercises
- Schedule enough time for Goodbye exercises such as shown in Chapter 3.4.

3.4 SAY HELLO - SAY GOODBYE EXERCISES – RITES OF PASSAGE

When teaching refugee children you have to be flexible because the length of time children will stay in your class varies enormously. Group dynamics will change all the time as children arrive and leave the group, a true challenge for every teacher.

Rites of passage are small rituals enabling teachers and children to support themselves and those around them in times of change. With a rite of passage you mark the transition to another phase of life. You express your gratitude for the old and you open yourself to embrace new beginnings. Saying hello and goodbye properly supports bonding between you and your pupils. When a child (or you yourself) is leaving, a thorough goodbye helps both of you to close your time together and to open up to new experiences.

hello/goodbye exercises
Three Say Hello - Say Goodbye exercises

1. Two Circles of Comfort
Say Hello: the children already in class form a circle, leaving an opening for the new children to enter through. They welcome the newcomers into their circle through the opening and then close the

circle. The newcomers form an inner circle. Children in the outer circle welcome the newcomers with kind words and compliments.

Say Goodbye: the outer circle is made up of the children who will stay in the class, the inside circle are the children who are leaving. The children who will be staying in the class thank the children in the inner circle for their talents and for the time they all spent together. The children who are leaving receive what is said to them and may want to share their feelings too. The outer circle opens and the inner circle children go on their way again.

2. The Book of Tips

Say Hello - Say Goodbye in one: every child who leaves the class to go to another school or country writes a piece of advice for newcomers in the Book of Tips. This is a simple and effective way for a child to express what they appreciated about the class, giving closure and allowing them to be open to the next phase in life. Some children may use their own language in the Book of Tips to make the new children feel even more welcome. As a teacher you make sure you understand what is written in the book by adding a translation, the children will enjoy helping you with this.

3. The Web of All Together

Say Hello: take a ball of wool and ask the children to make a circle. The teacher tosses the ball of wool to a child while holding onto the end of the thread. The children then toss the ball to others in turn, expressing what they wish for the newcomer. This exercise creates a web of good wishes, a warm welcome and a sense of connectedness. At the end of the exercise the web is placed carefully on the floor. Have the children take a photo or make a drawing about the web to help continue the feeling of all being together throughout the school year.

Trauma-sensitive teaching

Say Goodbye: take a ball of wool and ask the children to make a circle. The teacher tosses the ball of wool to a child while holding onto the end of the thread. This time the children express what they have appreciated about other children and what they have learned from being in the class. It is important to consciously lay down the web at the end of the exercise. Give the children the opportunity to keep a piece of the thread to take with them on their next step in life.

Extra exercise:

How would the children themselves like to say goodbye? You can introduce this topic by discussing what happens when people are saying goodbye. Ask about which thoughts and emotions they think may arise and how they wish to engage with them.

3.5 TOOLS FOR TRAUMA-SENSITIVE TEACHING

Every pedagogical tool that applies to regular education, applies to teaching refugee children as well. You just include extra warmth, compassion and patience.

A. Structure and predictability

structure and predictability

It seems obvious, but structure and predictability in the classroom help children to feel more grounded. They are able to trust and to feel safe because of schedules and rules. From this position children are willing to open up to new things like learning a new language, trying new food and adjusting to new habits.

- Put the daily plan on the board with images indicating play time, maths, cooking etc.
- Really start at 9 a.m. instead of subconsciously waiting for latecomers. It is only fair that the children who did arrive at school on time are rewarded for that, and it could inspire latecomers to try to be on time the next day as well.

- Start and end every day with games and talks about feelings and emotions. When a child's mind is burdened with worries and pain it is not possible for him to open up to learning... Having time to vent makes it easier for the child to participate in class. See also 3.5 Rituals and Life Skills Class. *time to vent*
- Restlessness is contagious but peacefulness is too: take advantage of the peace provided by structure and predictability.
- Clear class management is the basis of a healthy pedagogical climate: work in a clean, tidy classroom (including the back shelf of the furthest cupboard), prepare your classes and follow up any on promises or agreements you make with children, parents and colleagues. *warm pedagogical climate*
- "Contact before contract": first build a warm bond with the child, then make the deals about what you expect from them and what they can expect from you...
- Focus more on group activities than on schooling methods. This allows children to grow on a social and emotional level, to feel part of a group again and to feel safe enough to explore new ways of learning cognitively (maths, English etc) as well.

Boundaries are important for enabling children to feel safe. If you find it difficult to set boundaries 'because of what the child has experienced' you may not give the child what they need... Clear boundaries focus on the behaviour of the child (not on the child as a person!) and help the child to feel connected to you. You care about them enough to show what the desired behaviour is. *gift of boundaries*

> **TIP** | *Are you a headteacher? You may find that one class/school needs more structure for the children while another may possibly benefit from more flexibility. Check the level of structure regularly and adjust where needed. Always tailor the education offered to what the children need to learn.*

B. Own language

own language Allow the children time to speak their own language at school. To be able to express themselves in their own language - during lessons as well as during breaks - is important for the emotional processing of new information and experiences.

> **EXAMPLE** | *"I ask pupils to put sentences on the board in their own language. This way helps them to understand the structure of the English language more easily. It is empowering for commitment as well as for class dynamics. Every child loves to talk (proudly) about his own language."*
> Refugee teacher based in Canada

C. Pair newcomers with a buddy

buddy time A buddy is a class mate or an older pupil who will welcome a new child into the class and show them the ropes at school. This helps the newcomer to feel safe at school and in class more quickly.

D. Positive Teaching

positive teaching It is vital to stay positive and to focus on what a child can do or learn. Naming high expectations inspires the child to take that one step more to enjoy his (new) talents.

E. Involve parents and caretakers

parental participation Parental participation is crucial for a child's success in their school career. When teaching refugee children you may face parents who are dealing with severe challenges within their family and personal lives. Refugees are simultaneously processing their (flight) experiences as well as building up a new (temporary) life while their child is in your school's care. Being aware of this may help you feel compassion for the enormous strength refugee parents need to have – day by day.

Parental participation is a two-way street. How involved are you as a teacher with the parents? Here are a few ideas:
1. Open lessons: encourage parents to bring their child into the classroom and to stay for a short while. Hold open days.
2. Invite parents into the class to talk about their hobbies or professions.
3. Be clear about what kind of parental involvement you are looking for:
    a. Is it just help to keep the classroom inspiring that you need, or would you prefer practical support with education as well? For example, parents coming in to read with the children.
    b. Are you looking for involvement with their own child's class or with the whole school?

BE AWARE Parental participation can be discouraged by children who feel ashamed about the (semi-)illiteracy of their parents. Adults are usually slower than children to pick up a new language.

NOUR | *Nour is a highly educated mother from Pakistan who is corrected by her 11-year-old son with an eye roll and a sigh: "Pffff, mum you don't know this. Just let me say it".*

F. Every lesson should include all of the six senses

You are probably already preparing your lessons so that they are tailor-made for the needs of the children. Do you include the six senses yet? Since children need to feel present and relaxed in order to learn – and relaxation is felt in the body and in the mind – working with the senses provides an extra tool to inspire the child to be present and open to learning. Furthermore, some people learn best by seeing school work, others by hearing or reading. By including the six senses you can involve everybody in your lesson.

six senses

SIGHT | an attractive, clean classroom and visible lesson plan

TOUCH | ask your pupils to put their hand on their heart and share what they feel inside when reading a text

SMELL | incense, oil with sticks, fresh flowers or fruit in the classroom provide a pleasant environment. Lavender scent is relaxing while the scent of an orange (or orange blossom) relieves stress and inspires children to become active and positive.

HEARING | play classical music when the children are entering the classroom for the day, it stimulates the brain to learn

TASTE | try this one minute exercise -> when children are eating their lunch, ask them to chew consciously with their eyes closed for one minute. Afterwards they will feel more relaxed and focused.

INTUITION | how do you work with your intuition in school?

> **TIP |** *The Raisin exercise in Part 8 Mindfulness for Refugee Children can be used as introduction to working with the senses.*

G. Connect learning with emotions

emotional scripting

Although more and more creative ways of teaching become available, emotional scripting (see Edutopia) deserves a special place in trauma-sensitive teaching. While learning, children go through several emotions in class. Robert Plutchik constructed a diagram of eight basic emotions: joy, trust, fear, surprise, sadness, disgust, anger and anticipation. If learning is only from the mind, classes can become boring. When you involve emotions (and social-emotional learning) in your lessons children will connect their body to their mind, therefore making more space for learning.

Why not include (some of) these emotions in your lessons to inspire children even more at school?

1. Joy: play happy music to inspire children to write a positive story about their day.
2. Anticipation: put the next assignment in a box and talk with the children about how it feels when you don't know what the assignment is yet.
3. Strength: show some videos from/about role models for refugee children. Ask the children who they admire and enjoy their strength while watching the videos. How can they use the talents of their role model in their own life today?

role models

I advise you to be sensitive about the emotions you choose. It is important for refugee children to also invoke feelings such as joy, happiness and strength in order to nourish themselves before dealing with painful feelings (Thich Nhat Hanh). See Edutopia weblink at the Sources for full article on emotional scripting.

H. First Aid Relaxation Kit

Children love to have a special place in the classroom where they can be silent for a while when they experience strong emotions. A First Aid Relaxation Kit helps them to calm themselves. The Kit can include things like a cuddly blanket, soothing (Spotify) music, mindfulness exercises (Mindfulness in the Classroom on YouTube), a lavender scent, finger puppets, tissues and cuddly toys. Fill the box together with the children. They will know exactly what they need for a time-out.

First Aid Relaxation Kit

lavender scent

Extra suggestion: include a clear plastic bottle filled with water and glitter (and glued shut). The child can shake the bottle and watch the glitter swirl and finally settle – it is very relaxing!

I. Art Classes

Have children draw or play out their thoughts and feelings. That way they can process intense experiences even if they are not able (or not

Art Classes

willing) to express them vocally. Making art in nature is a wonderful way for children to receive the healing of nature (in Japan emerging in nature is called shinrin-yoku - 'forest bathing') combined with expressing themselves emotionally.

J.   Speak slowly

speak slowly   Learning a new language in school whilst processing uprooting experiences at the same time may take its toll on refugee children. Your clear articulation and your soft, slow voice helps them to understand the new language more easily.

K.   Importance of healthy nutrition

eat healthy   If at all possible take care of children's nutrition. To what extent this is possible will depend on where you are teaching. A child needs fresh vegetables and healthy food to be able to process their experiences and to open themselves to learning. Be careful with sugar because it may give children a short burst of energy. The health risks of sugar are well known. If for any reason a child does not receive (enough) proper food, please bear this in mind when the child has concentration issues in class…

L.   Do you ask a refugee child about his journey?

journey of the child   There is no conclusive advice on this matter. You could feel that holding back and not asking about the flight at all so as to avoid awakening painful emotions would be best. However, you could also choose to leave it up to the child to share anything they want to with you whenever they wish to. Remember that some refugee children will have arrived in their new homeland by plane for a family reunification. These children will have had a totally different experience to children who walked thousands of miles to reach their new homeland.

If children remember something during a group activity it can be healing for them to talk about the memory or to cry over it with the support of the group. It can be difficult for children when they feel as if there is no space to talk about their journey when they want to. It could feel like part of the teacher-pupil bond is missing. Just leave it up to the child and let your social support team know if you hear anything that needs follow up in the best interest of the child.

> **NOTE |** *Invest in a personal support team for yourself as well. If you are touched by the story of a child, take time to unwind and find support from colleagues or friends. It is vital that you take time to process your emotions as this reduces the risk of burnout.*

personal support team

M.   Intake talks with parents

It is important for children that you as a teacher know their history. Besides information about their previous schooling you need to know about the physical and emotional backgrounds of your new pupils. For example, if the child has visible scars you should know how they were inflicted. Ask the parents during an intake interview about the background of the child. It can be difficult and some parents do not want to share information about the child 'because we are in a new situation now, a new life'. However, the old life forms the foundations for the new life, if we do not know what the foundations look like it hard to build on them. Explaining that you need the information to guide their child as well as possible may help them to open up.

background information

N.   Hang a world map in your classroom

It helps children to feel more at home if they can literally see in which place they are right now. If they can see where they came from, where they travelled through and where their current home is this will support their grounding. Connecting their country of origin with their new (temporary) homeland can be supported if the child can point out the route they travelled on a map.

world map

Of course this is only appropriate if the child feels safe enough (or is old enough) to do so. Should a child become emotional this can give you a new opportunity for deeper understanding of that child. What touches him when he's thinking about his homeland? What does she miss most? Is there anything about what they miss that can also be found here? For example, making your own hummus like you did in Syria can (temporarily) relieve feelings of homesickness. If a child feels that they can show their emotions they will feel more at ease in class.

O. Classical music

YouTube and Spotify

YouTube and Spotify are your new best friends! Remember to play classical music while the children are entering the classroom for the day or need some help focusing. Listening to music and dancing is good for the soul, classical music especially may reduce stress symptoms and aid relaxation.

P. The power of ritual

power of ritual

Rituals are gatherings with the children that offer structure in another way... The old way is gone, the transitional phase (in which you are open to new insights) is here, the new phase is slowly starting. Rituals such as starting the day together in a circle are simple and easy.

The old = what happened before school
The transition = leave your worries behind and try to be totally present here in the circle
The new = now you are ready to start the school day

The same applies to the circle at the end of the day
The old = what happened today at school
The transition = leave what happened at school today behind and be totally present here in the circle
The new = now you are ready to go home

Energetic cleaning and charging

Try to clean the classroom after every school day, both physically (by sweeping, washing and wiping) and energetically. Energetic cleansing is removing the energy of what happened in the classroom that day and preparing the classroom for next day's lessons. Energetic cleansing can be done by phrasing your intention: 'May all negative and unnecessary energies leave this room'. Clean by opening the windows or using incense or a feather.

energetic cleansing and charging

Energetic charging of the classroom for the next day can be done by phrasing: 'From tomorrow morning this classroom will be filled with new, fresh energy to inspire all inside to have a fruitful, fulfilling day of learning.' Charge with wind, using another stick of incense or a second feather. Clean the tools (sweeping brush, cloths, incense, feather etc.) afterwards so that they are ready for next time.

Q. Mandala

Drawing or colouring a mandala helps the mind and heart to feel joy and to focus and relax. Mandala means holy circle in Sanskrit. The circle is a symbol of eternity and wholeness. The symmetrical forms within the circle help both children and adults to reflect and to recharge. With colours and different materials children (and teachers) can create beautiful art work to help the soul find a place to rest.
Use Google to find 'print mandalas for kids'.

Google: mandalas for children

R. Life Skills Class

A daily or weekly Life Skills Class supports the children to process their emotions and to learn about life's challenges and how to deal with them. The Hero's Journey as described in Chapter 4 is a suitable topic for this class. The same applies to inviting children to engage in social-emotional learning programs where they learn about issues such as emotions, feelings of self-worth and perspectives on the future.

Life Skills Class

teachingrefugeechildren.com

Social-emotional learning means learning about yourself as well as about your relationships with the people around you. The more familiar you are with your inner world, the more harmonious your contacts with others can be. This enhances feelings of well-being and strengthens life skills such as trust and persistence.

Prepared for the future
A Life Skills Class is a practical way to help refugee children build a solid foundation in themselves so that they can prepare themselves for the future knowing that whatever happens they will be able to cope with life's circumstances.

life skills

Less acting out
When children are aware that there will be time to talk about feelings, they may act out less during the day. Simply knowing that there will be time to vent what they are experiencing will help them to regulate their emotions more easily. In Life Skills Classes children have to actively participate while learning a lot about their inner life. Their improved self-understanding leads to more harmony in class and more empathy for classmates. Be aware that active participation can be challenging for pupils who are only used to listening passively to their teacher.

less acting out

inner and outer harmony

> Life Skills Classes are the perfect environment to explore the value of relationships.
>
> *"... school and most importantly the relationships formed at school can be an incredibly stabilising, positive and nurturing experience in a child's or a student's life, which can help them move on from more challenging times."*
> UNHCR Teaching About Refugees – Guidance on working with refugee children struggling with stress and trauma. For weblink see Sources.

TIP | *Drawing the eternity symbol or walking out its shape helps to process feelings and find solutions. Start with a question in your mind, walk or trace the shape of the symbol for a few minutes. Experience how you feel and think afterwards.*

S. Teaching in nature

Children love to be taught in nature. Take your children outside for lessons whenever possible. The power of the trees and grass or sand is healing. Everybody becomes more relaxed in nature and this opens children to learning. Make sure to offer the children a structure such as a clear circle on the ground (made with plants, stones or simply a length of rope) to help them focus where to sit and where to wander around or play.

teaching in nature

See website of Mikros Dounias for more inspiration about educational activities in nature (weblink at Sources).

T. Mindfulness

How can you help a child to focus their mind again after so much time in chaos? Mindfulness consists of practical concentration, attention and self-reflection exercises that you can apply directly in your classroom. With this approach you can further strengthen the pedagogical climate in your class. As one of the founders of modern mindfulness, Jon Kabat-Zinn, says: "Mindfulness is giving attention in the here and now, without judgment." By applying mindfulness exercises, traumatised or stressed children can discover moments of relaxation step by step. All exercises are best learned in the presence of a social care worker who will be able to guide the deeper emotions and feelings which can arise when a child relaxes. Using mindfulness,

see also Part 8 Mindfulness

children can slowly become familiar with their body and emotions again. By learning to observe experiences instead of acting or reacting to them, children learn how to regulate themselves. In this way they gain control of their behaviour at their own pace. This helps the children to feel safer and less tense. Mindfulness can also provide support if a child is distracted by his own thoughts a lot.

YOUTUBE | In the Sources at the end of this book you will find links to various mindfulness exercises in English - Arabic - Greek - Dutch.

One Minute Mindfulness exercises for teacher and child

one minute mindfulness

These are practical exercises that you can use today, or any day, before you start lessons.

For all exercises the suggestion is: switch phones off and make sure you will not be disturbed. Ask the children to close their eyes or to look at the table or at the floor. As a teacher, keep your eyes open for the children's sense of safety.

The exercises work best in a clean and quiet room. Choose one exercise each day and practice it for a few minutes to give your class more concentration. Having a class breathe in and out for half a minute at the beginning of a lesson gives pupils the opportunity to 'arrive' in your lesson. At the same time it gives you time to put your things down and be ready to start work calmly.

TIP | If you estimate that these exercises may unsettle some pupils, take these children to one side in advance. If you explain the setup so that they can feel more involved. Then your lesson may go more smoothly.

One Minute Mindfulness

1. Listen to the silence around you for one minute.
2. Imagine you have come from Mars and have never seen a pen before. Look at your pen for one minute.
3. Feel how firmly your feet rest on the floor, for one minute.
4. Smile to yourself for one minute.
5. Smile at your neighbour for one minute.
6. Walk in silence through the corridor for one minute.
7. Run for one minute.
8. Taste your drink consciously for one minute.
9. Have children look at nice picture on the board for one minute. Remove or cover the picture and ask them to draw it.
10. Count how often you exhale in one minute.

In the UNHCR manual 'Teaching About Refugees – Guidance on working with refugee children struggling with stress and trauma' you will find more suggestions as well as practical exercises to help children deal with stress and trauma. See weblink at Sources.

IMPORTANT | *You are a teacher not a therapist. Please refer children to a mental health practitioner or social care team if you think they need help.*

refer to mental health practitioner

3.6 SPECIAL ATTENTION FOR UNACCOMPANIED MINORS

unaccompanied minors

Children (under 18) travelling alone from their homeland to a new place are called unaccompanied minors. They deserve our special attention. Sometimes these children lost their parents during the journey or they may have been sent to prepare for the rest of the family coming. Bearing the burden of having to make a dangerous journey all by yourself is very hard. It means:
- Finding people who want to help you on your flight – on your own
- Contacting or becoming victim of human traffickers – and being alone
- Danger of being abducted and/or (sexually) abused and/or being sold to the highest bidder – without anyone to protect you
- Going through complicated asylum procedures in foreign languages – alone
- Finding your way in a new homeland – without parental support

Unaccompanied minors are extra vulnerable

extra vulnerable

The number of children travelling alone has risen in recent years. If you teach unaccompanied minors please make sure that there is a guardian or caretaker available for them through the channels in your country.

More and more refugee children are travelling alone
In recent years, the number of children migrating unaccompanied by guardians has increased. In 2015-2016, there were five times as many children estimated to be migrating alone than in 2010-2011 (UNICEF, 2017b). The number of unaccompanied and separated children applying for asylum in countries other than in the European Union increased from 4,000 in 2010 to 19,000 in 2015 (UNICEF, 2017b).
According to Eurostat, the number of unaccompanied minors among asylum seekers in Europe increased from 10,610 in 2010 to 95,208 in 2015, and then decreased to 63,280 in 2016.
Migration Data Portal

3.7 SUMMARY OF DO'S FOR POWERFUL GUIDANCE OF REFUGEE CHILDREN

summary of 7 do's

1. **Pay attention to your self-care (!)** and respect your boundaries while listening to children's stories about their experiences. Is self-care already regularly included on the agenda of your team meetings?

2. It is important to **interpret signals from children carefully**. That seems obvious but if 11-year-old Yara says nothing for a day, what do you do? The Dutch Speech Therapy Association advises that you accept silent periods from pupils. Yara does not say anything but remembers everything that you tell her. Does she understand what you ask her? Then her language development is going the right way!

interpretation of signals

3. Many newcomers **pick up language better in a classroom** than individually with a teacher. Why? Because they prefer not to be different - and they might feel different when they are taken out of a classroom setting.

4. **Choose your examples carefully** because an accident is sometimes caused by a tiny detail. A teacher asked Mo (aged 7) to add up boats during a maths lesson. Mo became so upset that he had to go home. The reason? The boy had travelled with his family from Africa to Europe by boat. When they had almost reached the shore they were forced to wait for days because no country would give them permission to land. They were running out of food and water. It was a traumatic experience for Mo. If the teacher had known this, they could have chosen another example.

5. **Self-regulation is a challenge for children with trauma.** Provide a silent place in the classroom or even a **First Aid Relaxation Kit** (see 3.5). A cuddly blanket, soothing (Spotify) music, mindfulness exercises (Mindfulness in the Classroom on YouTube), a lavender

self-regulation

scent. Fill the box together with the children. They will know exactly what they need for a time-out.

trauma is universal

6. **Experiencing trauma is universal** - everyone has their own challenges in life. What was a flight for one person may be the pain of a divorce for someone else. If you look at the experiences of newcomers with compassion, teaching becomes more equal. Not every refugee is (heavily) traumatised, they have a personal story - just like everyone else.

compassion

7. Refugee children and their parents f**eel instinctively when you are aware of and have compassion and understanding for what they have experienced.** You do not even have to talk to them about it. They sense your knowledge and warmth. Many times this provides openings for personal contact. This speeds up the feeling of being at home in your class.

> *"I want to live life, just like everybody else does."*
> Refugee child, 16

before you continue...

TIP | *Finally, before you continue, wait a moment. Do not turn this page yet, take a minute for your self-care. Breathe in and out a few times and look out of the window for a minute.*

3.8 WHAT WE SOMETIMES DO NOT THINK ABOUT... *attention!*
Teacher, it is so quiet!

These remarks and experiences of refugee children could easily be missed in class:
- During the first weeks in his new class a Syrian boy said: "Teacher, it is so quiet here, I don't hear bombs anymore".
- The sound of an electrical pencil sharpener can sound like a machine gun.
- The testing of the air raid alarm (as is done on the first Monday of every month at 12.00 in the Netherlands) or having a fire drill at school can cause immense fear in refugee children.
- Children and parents may have been travelling for years and/or have been moved up to 7 (!) times within their new homeland before they received permanent housing.
- It is not advised to introduce the Diary of Anne Frank to (new) refugee children in class.
- If a child had been on their knees for a long time on a boat during their flight they were possibly not able to walk for a while once ashore. Knee bending exercises during gym lessons may cause these memories to resurface. *careful with knee bending exercises*
- If a child is afraid of the toilet maybe they weren't allowed to drink before the boat trip...
- Be aware of conspiracy thinking if there was no freedom of press in the country of origin. Children may have lived in a war zone while seeing propaganda on television insisting that there was peace/nothing going on in their country.
- If the child is used to praying in order to relax or to manage their anxiety, you might consider joining them in prayer. If this is at odds with your own religion, just sitting next to the child in silence may help them feel connected, supported and safe. *silent company*
- 8-year old Khaled lived in a basement in Aleppo, there was bombing all around them. He and his siblings had to be silent when there were snipers in the street. Now that he is safe in Belgium Khaled still refuses to speak.

The Hero's Journey – Rites of Passage

PART 4

"When you follow your bliss, and by bliss I mean the deep sense of being in it, and doing what the push is out of your own existence—it may not be fun, but it's your bliss and there's bliss behind pain too... You follow that and doors will open where there were no doors before, where you would not have thought there'd be doors, and where there wouldn't be a door for anybody else." ~From The Hero's Journey

From Joseph Campbell's The Hero's Journey Copyright
© Joseph Campbell Foundation (jcf.org) 2014. Used with permission.

TAGS

Steps of The Hero's Journey | Call to start | Crossing the threshold | Encountering ordeals and helpers | Finding the treasure | Reconciliation with the new | Crossing the threshold again | Another call awaits

Teaching Refugee Children

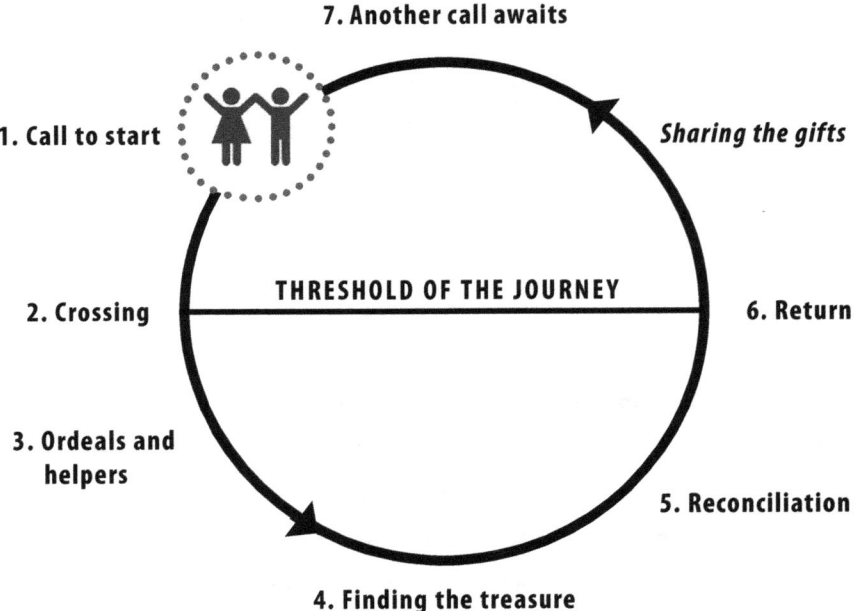

Hero's Journey ® Schema

"Joseph Campbell's Hero's Journey schema from The Hero with a Thousand Faces (New World Library) copyright © 2008 by the Joseph Campbell Foundation (jcf.org), used with permission."

> With deep gratitude for the work of Joseph Campbell. His dedication to providing us with a universal, archetypal model of growing the soul has been a warm inspiration in writing this book. May you too feel supported on your personal hero journey in life.

4 | THE HERO'S JOURNEY – RITES OF PASSAGE

INTRODUCTION THE HERO'S JOURNEY

The soul goes through experiences in its life that you could compare with the experiences of heroes in myths. The American Joseph Campbell was a mythologist who compared mythology and religion from around the world. He described the life long journey of the soul from a psychological point of view, in his book The Hero with a Thousand Faces. Everyone has the ability to make this journey in their own way, time, and form.

The journey provides you with opportunities to leave life as you know it behind, discover hidden talents in yourself, return with your unique gifts and share them in the world. It is a psycho-spiritual model of the growth many of us are making. On a conscious, as well as on an unconscious level. When you look at your work as a refugee teacher from this perspective it can give you an idea of where the child is at and how you can support him or her to the best of your abilities.

In this chapter Joseph Campbell's Hero's Journey is applied especially for refugee teachers and refugee children. This journey is divided into 7 steps, which can be found in the model below. Each step describes what it entails, how it can be recognised in the life of a refugee child and how you can guide the child in that step. The steps or phases may partly overlap or arise as a result of another step.

1. Call to start the journey
2. Crossing the threshold into the unknown
3. Encountering ordeals and helpers/mentors
4. Finding the treasure: letting go of the old and welcoming rebirth
5. Reconciliation with the new life
6. Crossing the threshold to the world with your unique gifts
7. Another call for a journey awaits

1. CALL TO START THE JOURNEY

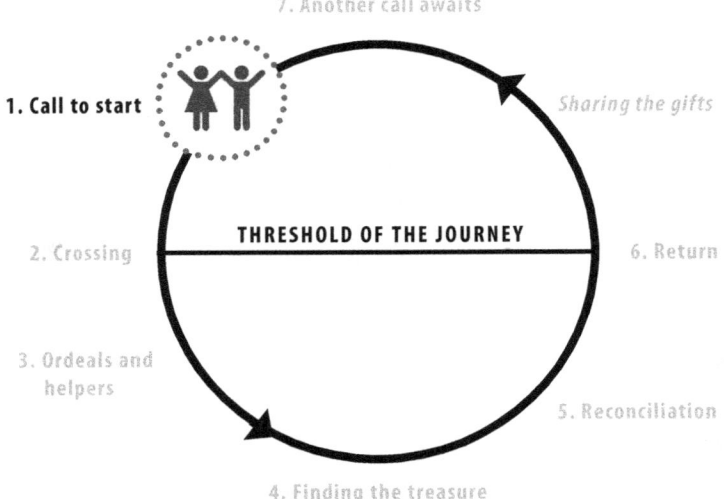

Every journey starts with the first step. What motivates or triggers you to take this first step? In situations of war or poverty parents have often tried to make the best of their life's circumstances for a very long time. Sometimes a war has started recently, in other cases children have been born during a civil war. When is the right time to leave one's old life behind and look for a safe place to live? This is a different calling for every person. The call to start the journey may be:

- Bombing nearing their home town
- The loss of home, work or basic security
- Discrimination because of ethnicity, sex or religion
- Poverty and hunger
- _____
- _____

Refugees experience a literal journey from their place of origin to a new (temporary) homeland. There is also the inner journey that every person can choose to take in their life. From a psychological point of view the call to start your inner journey may be 'signs' showing you that changes are needed in order to help you fulfil your new deep

The Hero's Journey – Rites of Passage

needs and wishes. These signs may come in different shapes and forms. To name just a few you can experience:

- Returning doubts or worries about whether your job, a friendship or a relationship still feels good for you
- Receiving an unexpected phone call
- Seeing something in a movie that strikes you and lingers with you for a while
- Returning thoughts about making a change in your life
- A sudden negative assessment at a job interview causing you stress

It is always up to you whether to act on the call. As you can see in the circle of the Hero's Journey: listening to the call will lead you to the decision whether or not to cross the threshold into the unknown. The unknown is the place where you can discover your hidden talents and gifts.

HOW TO NOTICE THIS STEP IN THE LIFE OF A REFUGEE CHILD?

CALL TO START | *Nadia's parents hoped that the war in Syria would be short. That was 3 years ago. They knew that if they fled to another country they would not be able to take her 90 year old grandmother with them. So, they waited and waited, hoping for better days. When the snipers started to come closer to their house in Aleppo and Nadia and her sister could no longer sleep at night because of the bombing, her parents made the decision to flee to Turkey. Hoping to reach Europe via Lesvos, Greece.*

GUIDING THE CHILD

For the teacher Can you name a situation that you left as a child because you instinctively sensed danger? It could be an experience when you were at primary school, playing outside with friends etc. Did you decide to leave or did your parents make that choice? How did you feel about that? Powerless, relieved, uncertain, anxious?

_____
_____

If you prefer to relate to your present life: How do you describe your call to start your (inner) journey towards teaching refugee children? Was it because of an inspiring colleague? Did your headmaster ask you to? Was it out of an innate interest in educating these special children? Did you feel an urge to participate in humanitarian work?

_____
_____

If possible, depending on the situation of the refugee children you are teaching, share your feelings and insights about personal experiences with feeling powerless with them on their own level. Explain to them that you have sometimes had to give up or leave behind something that you loved in order to take the next step in your life. They may well be inspired to open up about why they started their journey.

For the child When educating children about listening to their instincts (acting on a call to start a journey) it is inspiring to use the seasonal migrations of birds as a metaphor. Use a world map for this exercise. Having a world map in the classroom also provides the children with structure and a warm connection to their birth country. Use the map to show how birds fly south for winter and north again when summer is coming (depending on your location you may want to use another example). Refugee children can relate to the migration of birds because they too are temporarily leaving their country because of a situation of shortage (war or poverty symbolise winter time). After this scarcity is over they might be able to return to their country (summer time).

Please work together with psychologists or social workers in this exercise.

2. CROSSING THE THRESHOLD INTO THE UNKNOWN

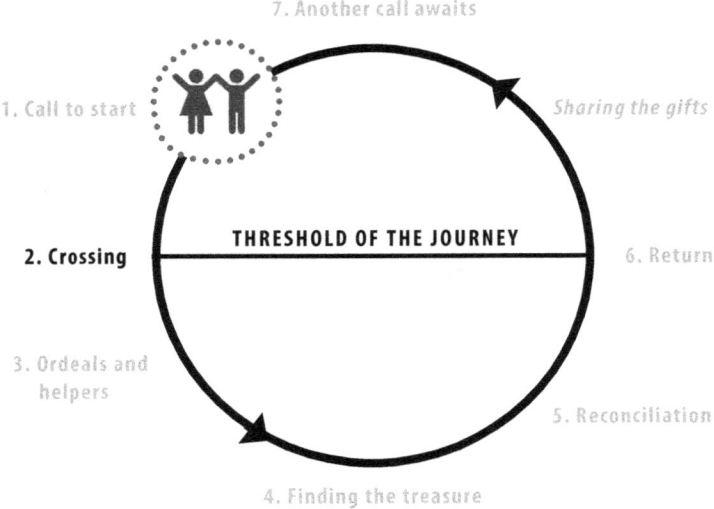

When parents decide to flee, a child has no choice but to go too. This forced upheaval can cause severe inner conflict for children. Their loyalty to their parents can be challenged by feelings of insecurity, intense fear of the unknown and being forced to surrender. The child could feel that their parents occasionally doubt their decision to flee. It is a painful decision to make but the best interests of the children is almost always a driving factor. However, when the better life will actually start is still unknown. Dealing with long periods of insecurity – such as waiting for a call from the smuggler to say it is time to cross into another country, or during an unclear asylum processes - is a very challenging factor in the lives of refugee families.

You need to be able to contain this insecurity. There may come a point in anyone's life that they know they have to change the situation they are in. Whether it be work, a relationship or (in this case) the country you no longer feel safe or at home in. The process of saying "no" to the old and "yes" to the new is likely to contain periods of doubt about the decision. Sometimes this transitional period takes a long time. One can't know beforehand how things will go. Crossing the threshold truly means taking a giant leap of faith into the unknown, hopefully one that leads to better circumstances. Trusting the process and allowing your feelings to come and go – instead of changing your mind when the going gets tough – is sometimes the only thing that people can do in this transitional phase. The old is gone and the new has not yet taken form. Transformation is exactly that. The changing of form with no guarantees that the new will be 'better' but with the inner knowledge that it will bring you closer to who you really are. Like a snake you must shed the old skin in order to renew yourself. Helpers and tests along the way will guide you to renewal, as we will see in the next step - step 3.

The art of patience

Patience is an essential part of the willingness to surrender yourself to the unknown. How you feel influences your behaviour. People can use the waiting time to, for example, practice patience in challenging times. The challenge will be there, how we deal with it is up to each and every one of us. Resistance may lead to more suffering and pain. Suffering, in its essence, is part of life. People experience suffering in the form of a broken heart, going bankrupt, getting ill, going through a difficult divorce or fleeing their home country as a refugee. There is no comparison in pain, it is a purely individual life phase. Once you are able to open up to the fact that pain is a part of life, have patience and trust that after each difficult phase a new phase will show itself this may help you go through emotional transitions in life.

HOW TO NOTICE THIS STEP IN THE LIFE OF A REFUGEE CHILD?

CROSSING THE THRESHOLD | *Nadia's father contacted a smuggler in Aleppo. He paid him € 5.000 ($ 5.850) to take his family to Istanbul, Turkey. On arrival in Istanbul the next smuggler he was introduced to told him to pay € 1.000 ($ 1.170) per person to make the crossing to Lesvos, Greece. Her father paid extra for access to a dinghy with a maximum of 20 people aboard. The smuggler told Nadia's father to go to the Turkish coast across from Lesvos and wait for a telephone call. The dinghy would cross the Aegean Sea only when the weather was safe. The money was already paid but it could take days or weeks before they would receive the phone call. Or, maybe, they wouldn't be called at all and would have lost all their money?*

The Hero's Journey – Rites of Passage

GUIDING THE CHILD

For the teacher What was your most intense experience while crossing a threshold into the unknown? Was it when you bought your plane ticket to travel to the refugee community you are currently working in? Maybe it was your decision to quit a job without having yet found new work? Or was it leaving a relationship knowing you are afraid to be on your own? How did you feel until you were comfortable with your changed circumstances?

_____
_____

For the child What can you do today to help the refugee children in your class process their feelings around dealing with the unknown?

_____
_____

Suggestion 1   Transformation Explain how a caterpillar turns into a beautiful butterfly. For the caterpillar the change may seem to be the end of the world, but for the butterfly it was necessary to have grown from caterpillar into beauty. There is little or no growth possible without pain, but there may well be a better life waiting for you after a big change.

connect past, present and future

Suggestion 2   Make a connection between past, present and future Have children make a drawing or write a song or a play about what they used to do back home, what they are doing now, in their new home, and what their dreams are for the future. This 'connection between lives' supports children to:
- Feel more grounded
- Learn to know their own identity
- Relate to classmates by discovering that we all share the same experiences in life

Please work together with psychologists or social workers in this exercise.

3. ENCOUNTERING ORDEALS AND HELPERS/MENTORS

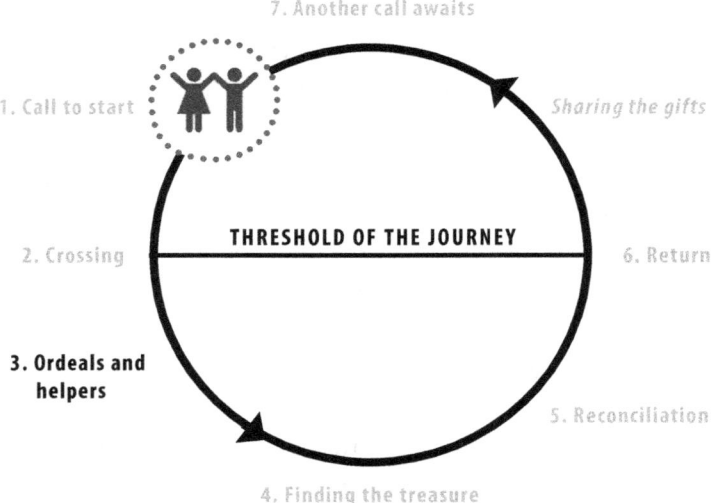

On the journey you will face challenges that test your strength and commitment to make a better life for yourself. An ordeal can be seen as a (sometimes very difficult) opportunity to grow your strength. You can also experience it as a temptation. A test to see if you go back to your old life or resist and continue with your plan to change your life. You will meet 'helpers' at the most unexpected moments. It might be someone who just says the right words at the right moment. Helpers can be people or help could come to you via a song you hear, a dream you have, a movie you see or even in the form of a memory, for example of a conversation you had years ago with someone and that suddenly comes to mind. Allow yourself to be open to receiving the right information at the right time to help you take the next step in your journey of personal growth.

The Hero's Journey – Rites of Passage

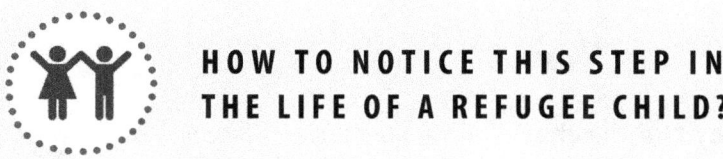

HOW TO NOTICE THIS STEP IN THE LIFE OF A REFUGEE CHILD?

TEMPTATION | *While the family were waiting in Istanbul Nadia's grandfather called. Their grandmother was feeling unwell and he pleaded with them to return to Aleppo to say goodbye to her. It was a heart breaking conversation. Nadia's father felt torn between the love for his parents and his determination to make a safer life for his children. With a heavy heart he chose to continue the journey to Europe. That night he had a dream about his mother, she was smiling about the new life of her son in Europe. Nadia's father felt relieved that he had made the right decision, no matter what insecurities would lie ahead of them.*

ORDEAL | *Two days after arriving at the Turkish coast the phone rang. The boat would sail early the next morning. Nadia remembers the smell of the crowd of people waiting to board. Her mother had not allowed her anything to eat or drink since the previous evening to be sure that she wouldn't need to relieve herself on the boat. Her belly hurt from the hunger and thirst. When they arrived at the beach her father saw that there were already 40 people on the boat. He complained that he had paid extra for a safer boat transporting only 20 people. The assistant smuggler pointed a gun at his head and made them board the boat. There was no turning back for Nadia's family.*

HELPER | *One of the other Syrian families on board asked the smuggler in Turkish to please have mercy on Nadia's family. The smuggler lowered his gun.*

GUIDING THE CHILD

For the teacher As in any story, there is a hero facing challenges along the path that leads to the treasure (in this case, a more fulfilled life). Which challenges and temptations have you experienced during your personal journey of change?

_____
_____

For the child Read the children suitable stories or fables that introduce the concept of ordeals/tests and helpers. Can your pupils identify the challenges and the helpers?
On http://www.taleswithmorals.com/ you will find Aesop's Fables.

fables

Please work together with psychologists or social workers in this exercise.

4. FINDING THE TREASURE: LETTING GO OF THE OLD AND WELCOMING REBIRTH

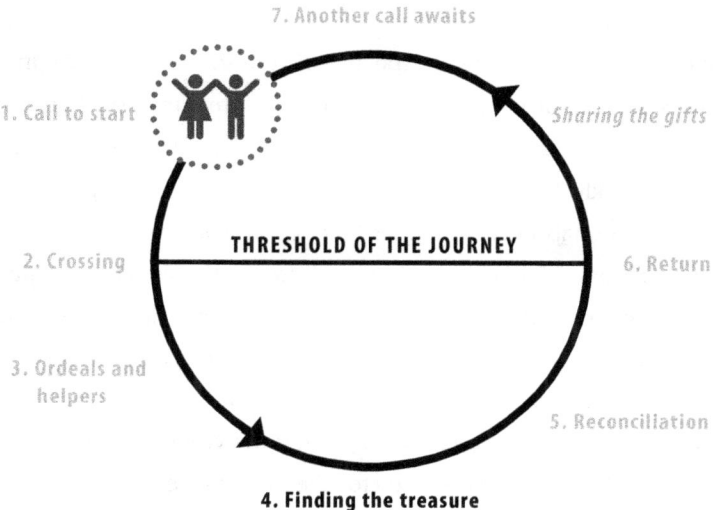

4. Finding the treasure

At this stage you have found new wisdom, insights and ideas that will enable you to make a new start. You will probably not go back to an old way of thinking because once the genie is out of the bottle you cannot go back to the way things were before. It is simply impossible to go back to not knowing once you know. Your newly gained knowledge will open so many doors for you that you will probably not wish to go back to earlier times.

As with the other stages of the journey, surrendering to the forces of life and of your soul is the way forward. The new insight or talent wants to be born. Trying to suppress, ignore or avoid this natural process is like trying to hold a ball under water. It will not work for long, the forces of nature insist the ball must float. The same applies to the journey of a soul wishing to travel.

Finding the treasure is an inner reconciliation with that which you had resisted earlier. Reconciliation with the fact that your soul expresses the desire to grow and that you sometimes have to leave old ways behind. This can be in ways that you would not choose but that need to happen in the broader perspective of your soul's growth. Insights - calls to start or continue your journey - sometimes start subtly. Maybe with an unpleasant remark from your boss that you want to forget quickly. However, if we ignore these insights for a period of time, the signals become louder. You get stomach pains when you see your boss. As soon as you begin to listen to the signal, it will give you directions and inspirations for your next step in life. Signals and insights may come in the form of remarks made by people, a word or sentence in a book, a movie or even in a dream. The signs are of and for your soul. They are there to help you grow. When you are able to welcome the signs you are ready to take the next step in your life.

The ultimate letting go and welcoming the new

For a refugee family, arrival in the new homeland may seem like the ultimate in letting go of the old and welcoming the new. This arrival is what they have worked so hard for and what they have wished for, for such a long time. They have found their treasure.

What might treasure look like?

Sometimes you realise that you have discovered a treasure that you were not actively seeking. Coincidently you feel more relaxed, experience a new perspective on matters or are not triggered by issues that could easily have consumed your energy earlier. This (sometimes subconscious) surrender to whatever life brings could be the treasure that your soul was looking for.

What if a refugee (child) is unhappy in their new homeland?

…sometimes expectations can be so high that you will be disappointed with what you receive. It may not seem like a gleaming golden treasure after all. But, it is still the new reality you have to deal with.

In these cases it may be helpful for the refugee (child) to talk about or write down a number of positive things that they do have now. Which treasures are available every day? For example, safety, food, shelter…This positive thinking (is the glass half full or half empty?) brings the mind to a more receptive state, allowing them to focus on what is there instead of focusing on what is missing. This will lead to more positive patterns of thinking. Just like the law of attraction, if you focus on scarcity that is probably what you will experience. Abundance thinking leads to experiencing abundance – for example enjoying warm rays of sunshine and may lead to receiving more unexpected experiences of abundance.

When expectations were too high a child can think…

- *Is this the promised land? So cold and with food I don't like?*
- *Why are we being threatened by locals?*
- *We have been waiting for years for asylum but it is totally unclear if and when we will get our answer.*

# HOW TO NOTICE THIS STEP IN THE LIFE OF A REFUGEE CHILD?

WELCOMING REBIRTH | *When Nadia finally arrived on the shores of Lesvos, Greece, she was brought to a beautiful shelter under the pine trees. There, the most vulnerable refugees were given time to heal while waiting for their asylum procedure. In the mornings she attended the 'school in nature'. Receiving education in the forest helped her to process her experiences in a gentle way. She was fond of the teachers and loved being able to go to school at the shelter. Close to her parents and together with other refugee children and Greek children. Every time Nadia felt homesick, she tried to write a Positive Thinking List. A List that quickly turned into a Positive Thinking Drawing!*

Today...I am wearing better clothes than I had on the dinghy.
Tomorrow...I will be the angel in our theatre performance in the city.
Now...the teacher smiles at me and my mother calls me for dinner.

The Hero's Journey – Rites of Passage

GUIDING THE CHILD

For the teacher

1. What treasures do you experience in your life? Make a Positive Thinking List and show it to the children.

2. What have you experienced as a breakthrough in your life so far? Was it meeting someone who changed your life in a profound way? Did you feel that you needed to make a firm decision and finally understand why you needed to make it?

_____

_____

Explaining the concept of life changing experiences to children may lead to the most wonderful stories and tales.

3. Tell the children how the lotus grows from mud into a beautiful flower. Or how a pearl is formed by a grain of sand irritating an oyster. Working with images like this helps children to stay hopeful for positive change. There is always a chance to heal your situation!

For the child

1. After showing the children your Positive Thinking List, ask them to make their own Positive Thinking List or Drawing. Ask them if you can share the lists with the class. Asking permission to share private information from children can be healing to them, especially for refugee children who have experienced a huge lack of privacy on their journey.

Google: planting seeds with kids

2. Plant seeds with children so that they can experience values such as love, dedication, nourishment and the laws of nature. Use seeds that sprout easily and clear containers so that the children can see the roots forming!

Source: https://craftulate.com/fast-growing-seeds-kids/

Please work together with psychologists or social workers in this exercise.

5. RECONCILIATION WITH YOUR NEW LIFE

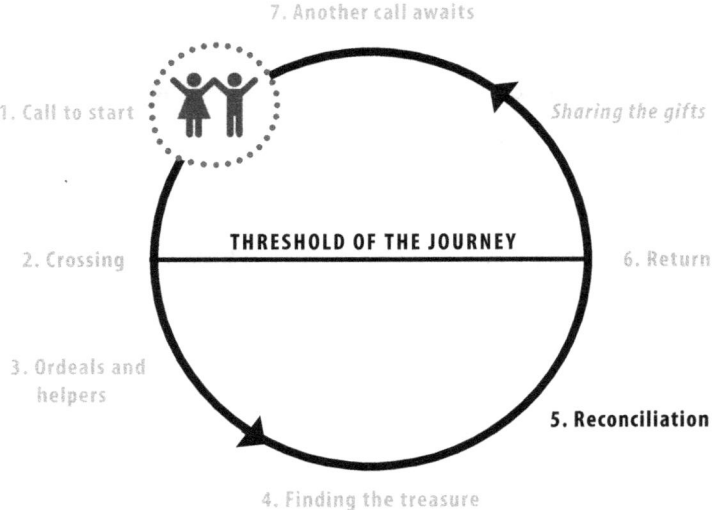

Making the best of life in a refugee camp or in your new homeland

A gift may look different than you had expected. Experiencing a long-term stay in a refugee camp does not have to mean that your life can only continue once you have been granted a new place, asylum. While it may be an ordeal for one refugee to wait (sometimes in severe hardship) for procedures to be completed or the end of a war, another refugee may feel that the camp is an improvement on their previous life. Regardless of their outer circumstances, he or she can share inner talents and gifts with those they are thrown together with. Inner growth continues. You can oppose something that doesn't take good care of you endlessly - a government, an NGO, the world... That is often the case but, also as a refugee, you can decide how you deal with your situation. This is a more mindful approach to life: we do not determine what happens in our lives but we are able to choose how we wish to deal with our circumstances.

Reconciling with your new life - however it looks - is crucial for inner peace. In the meantime, you can take the freedom to see where you can develop yourself further. This can be as mundane as practicing patience while waiting in line for your food. You can choose to keep resisting this experience because you used to live in abundance, but is also an opportunity to ask 'how can I get the best out of myself in this situation?'

HOW TO NOTICE THIS STEP IN THE LIFE OF A REFUGEE CHILD?

RECONCILIATION | *Nadia loved planting seeds and watching them grow into healthy food and beautiful flowers. Her connection to the earth helped her to relax and to connect with her new life. She was dedicated to taking care of her small garden at the refugee shelter.*

GUIDING THE CHILD

For the teacher What can you share with your pupils regarding gifts you found after a breakthrough in your life and how you use those gifts? It is inspiring to explore examples of situations that seemed difficult and how you found a silver lining within them.
For example: you were out of work but had more time to see your friends, write a book or to be thankful for the little things you had

_____
_____

For the child Ask them to make a drawing, write a poem or write a song about silver linings in their life.

Please work together with psychologists or social workers in this exercise.

6. RETURN TO THE WORLD WITH YOUR UNIQUE GIFTS

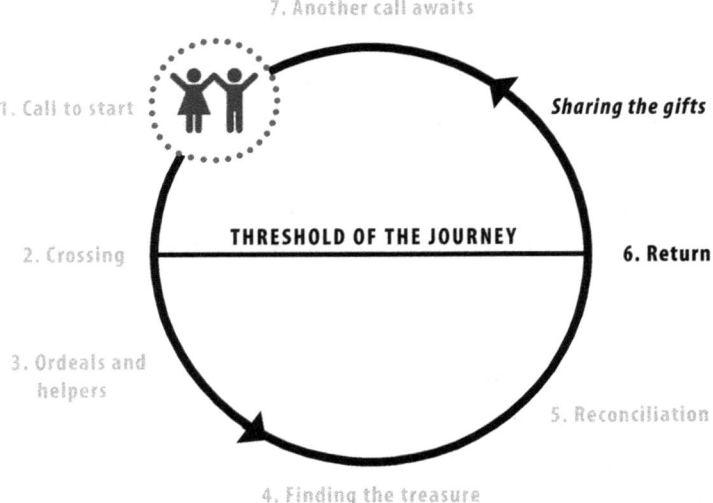

Share your gifts

Once again you cross the threshold. This time to return to daily life and share your gifts: your new insights and experiences. You share them with people in similar situations to improve the world. You no longer keep your thoughts or new ideas to yourself but offer them to like-minded people so they too can broaden their perception of life.

It is called a threshold because in this step you need determination and courage to stand up for what you have discovered. You will meet people who do not understand what you are talking about. They may have known you in the past and don't share your ideas or way of thinking anymore. Maybe they will mock you or try to hinder you. Please know that these tests are an important part of the journey. It is called a hero's journey for a reason! You need the courage to plainly offer what you wish to share and to keep moving on authentically.

Don't try to convert people or organisations to your new way of thinking. Just put your idea on the table as if it is a pen. Then lean back. If the other person is interested they will take the pen. If not, someone else will. Maybe at another time in another place. It's as simple as that.

HOW TO NOTICE THIS STEP IN THE LIFE OF A REFUGEE CHILD?

THRESHOLD | *Nadia was not sure what her unique talents were. She thought she was nothing special and just went along with things as they happened. One day her teacher, Peter, asked the children about their unique gifts to the world. Nadia made herself small and avoided the teacher's eyes; hoping she wouldn't have to answer his question. Bad luck.... Peter stood in front of Nadia and gently asked her about her talents.*
'I don't have any', she whispered.
'What are your hobbies, what do you most like to do?' the teacher asked.
'I like to sing and dance. I also like to paint.' Nadia was more enthusiastic when she could talk about her favourite things to do.
'How about your little garden?' asked Peter.
How could she have forgotten her garden... Of course, that was a passion of hers as well.
'Maybe your hobbies are your talents?' Peter suggested.
Nadia needed some time to think about the possibility that she had talents too. She felt her heart opening up. 'Yes', she sighed, 'these are my talents.'

GUIDING THE CHILD

For the teacher How do you deal with resistance in your life? When was the last time you tried to convince someone to be open to what you stand for?

_____

_____

Share your findings with your class and playfully teach the children about the value of inner knowledge, commitment to yourself and elegantly letting go when something turns out differently to how you had envisaged. This will empower the children to stay true to themselves no matter how the outside world may react.

_____

_____

For the child Children who think they are not talented might open up if you ask them what they like to do most. If they can do what makes them happy (singing, dancing, gardening, drawing etc) it opens their hearts and this might make it slightly easier for them to process their experiences.

beautiful talents

If a child is unable to share anything about their hobbies you can also ask: what advice would you give a new child who has just joined the class? The suggestion(s) may reveal hidden talents such as compassion, social or organisational skills, humour and creativity.

Please work together with psychologists or social workers in this exercise.

7. ANOTHER CALL FOR A JOURNEY AWAITS

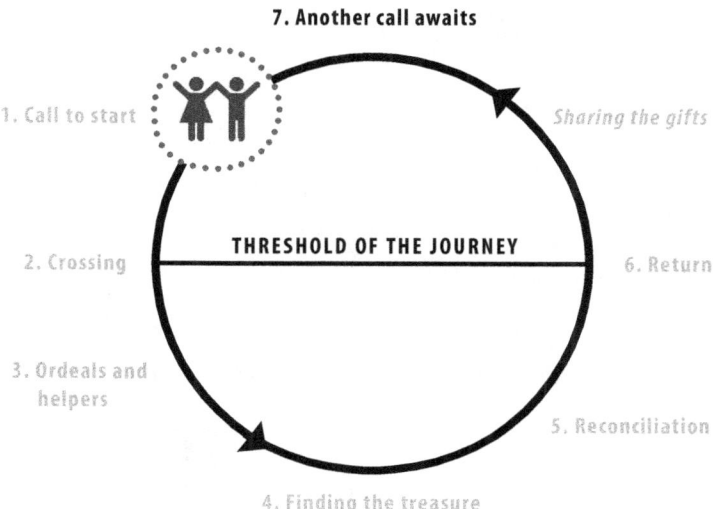

Since your soul wishes to continue growing, there will come a time when you are ready to enter the next circle of change. New ideas or impulses may arise. This is how you know you are ready to embark on a new journey. The more times you have supported yourself with the Hero's Journey model, the easier changes in life will be for you.

Each time you will recognise what is working for you and what is ready for change at an earlier stage. Like a caterpillar turning into a butterfly. Subtle thoughts, dreams and encounters may inspire you to renew your views on aspects of your life. You will not need the hard bang of resistance anymore. You will feel a change is necessary and you will probably act on it. Good luck on your new journey.

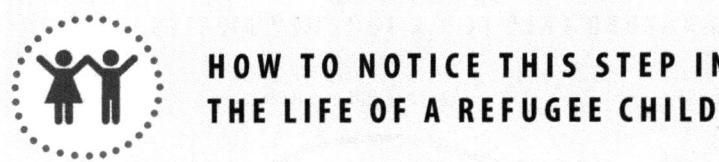

HOW TO NOTICE THIS STEP IN THE LIFE OF A REFUGEE CHILD?

ANOTHER CALL FOR A JOURNEY | *Nadia was content with her daily visits to her garden. Slowly she taught other children how to grow seeds too. One day Nadia's teacher asked her if she would like to make a video tutorial about her gardening tips. He would upload the video to YouTube so other children could benefit from Nadia's experience.*

A new call for a journey has arrived!

GUIDING THE CHILD

For the teacher Share an experience of a new change after a (big) change. What made you think about change? What triggered you most? A conversation? A movie? Something you read in a book? Draw the Hero's Journey on the blackboard and explain your steps. Briefly summarise your last change and introduce the start of the next journey you wish embark upon!

_____
_____

For the child Have children draw the journey of the sun across the sky. Use the phases to explain the seasons in life.

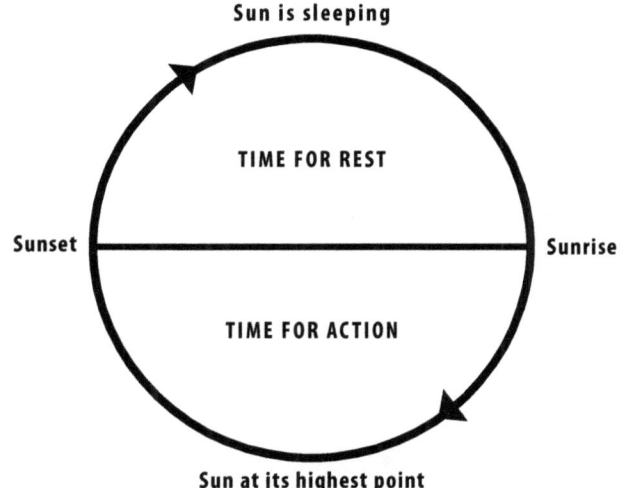

Sunrise = start of an idea
Sun at its highest point = the idea comes to life
Sunset = where you evaluate how the idea has worked out
Sun is sleeping = where you relax and rest before a new idea pops into your mind

Please work together with psychologists or social workers in this exercise.

NOTES

Refugee children advising teachers

PART 5

"*If you tell us a little about your life, it makes it easier for me to share a little about mine.*"

Refugee child

TAGS

colourful clothes | patience please | mother tongue say my name

5 | REFUGEE CHILDREN ADVISING TEACHERS

The best advice comes from the children themselves!

1. "Talk with us instead of just giving us knowledge."
2. "Ask us what we need instead of sticking too much to the school curriculum. We have encountered experiences in life that make us critical about what we think we need to learn in school."
3. "Please wear colourful clothes, you can brighten up our day by looking nice. It makes us feel that you have made an effort to make us happy." *colourful clothes*
4. "Start and finish the class on time, we like the structure of the school day."
5. "If you tell us a little about your life, it makes it easier for me to share a little about mine."
6. "Have patience with us and please be kind. A smile can brighten our day!" *patience please*
7. "I understand that you don't speak or understand our language but please give us space to speak our mother tongue. It helps us to process feelings and get ready for another language class!" *mother tongue*
8. "We like to learn about the country we are (temporarily) staying in. If teachers could include that in the lessons we would feel more at home."
9. "Please treat me as if I am your own child."
10. "We like to go to school, please make sure that there are enough teachers for us. We don't understand when someone promises us that we can go to school but then informs us that we can't as there are not enough teachers."

	11. "We understand that you might have had a bad day before you came to school but we would appreciate it if you could try to be friendly to us…"
mindfulness
say my name	12. "I love it when I hear you pronouncing my name correctly. It feels like home to me."
13. "I understand that I have to follow classes that are below my level of intelligence and that I am obliged to follow them to learn the new language. Meanwhile I am still processing traumatic experiences and at the same time building up my new life. Please give me time and peace and provide me with educational projects that I am allowed to do in my own language. You may be surprised by the outcome of my work!"

NOTES

Refugee teachers advising teachers

PART 6

"Seeing the person behind the refugee is crucial for real contact. I have a lot of respect for the strength of the pupils now that I have seen what they experienced along the way."

Refugee teacher

TAGS

critical pupils | help them to 'land'| school protocol can change | to flee or to migrate | singing lullabies

6 | REFUGEE TEACHERS ADVISING TEACHERS

The following quotes from refugee teachers in Europe may inspire you too.

1. "Refugee children are coming to school because they have to, not necessarily because they want to. Especially refugee children in secondary education may have had such life changing experiences (smugglers, poverty, cold, hunger, abuse) that they can be extra critical about what they wish to learn. Engage with them on an equal basis and let them know that you are aware of their past. Talk with them about their wishes in education to get them on board." *critical pupils*
2. "I realise that we are all connected and I use The Web of All Together-exercise." (Chapter 3.4)
3. "I tell my (refugee) children how important education is. That you can learn through education about there being other opinions and stories than those you already know. They all nod in agreement when they realise they learn so much more at school than a language or profession."
4. "I think our role should be to get children to 'land', to help them find how they can be themselves again. That is something we can do at school, by teaching our pupils skills that will benefit them for the rest of their lives. Not by denying what they have experienced, but by looking at how they can move on." *help them to 'land'*
5. "Because I travelled to Greece, I know a bit more about their flight. As a result, I have a different approach to starting a conversation with pupils. I have more appreciation for the resilience of the children and I do not mind anymore if they fall asleep during the day. One of my pupils thanked me for having visited Lesvos: 'How wonderful that you want to understand us.'"

structure

6. "We have adapted the school protocol: at the beginning of the school year we do more games for group formation and trust building. Every time a newcomer arrives we pick up those group games again. This way the class remains a safe community."

7. "Refugee children had unpleasant associations with emergency services, many became very panicked when they saw people in uniform or heard ambulances. We have invited emergency services such as police and ambulance to the schoolyard to help rewrite associations."

8. "Seeing the person behind the refugee is crucial for real contact. I have a lot of respect for the strength of the pupils now that I have seen what they experienced along the way."

9. "Refugee children can feel like a burden or a guest in their new (temporary) country. After I became more immersed in the background of the children, they asked me 'teacher, do you now have more appreciation for us as refugees?'"

10. "Visit a refugee reception location in your city, contact with refugees is not as scary as you think."

11. "Let's not forget the fathers in parent conversations. They also need a listening ear."

12. "Children need time. Sometimes we think 'it does not work' too quickly but we should give the child more time to land after so much chaos and mistrust during the long journey."

TIP | Are children hyper aware in class? Or starting arguments about the smallest details? This day curriculum can be helpful:
- Play time with water/sand/play dough/free painting
- A bit of working
- Lunch break
- Singing (mother tongue) lullabies to relax (this also works for secondary school)
- Individual play or work

power of lullabies

NOTES

Universal values in practice

PART 7

*"We are all connected in one long chain,
helping refugee children in every country along the way."*

Volunteer in a refugee community in Europe

TAGS

universal values | cultural history | understanding of cultures
confidence | exercises for teachers | school directors

7 | UNIVERSAL VALUES IN PRACTICE

7.1 INTRODUCTION

When working with refugee children universal values offer a strong tool in connecting with the child. As I mentioned in my book Connecting Values, Multicultural Guidance for Primary Education: "Values rise above educational, language, political, cultural and social-economical differences. It doesn't matter where someone is from or how they think. When your focal point is the values you share it is possible to connect easily: surely everybody wants to be happy and to create a better life for themselves."

universal values

verbindendewaarden.nl

In this chapter you will find practical exercises to implement the universal values Connection - Trust - Compassion for yourself and for your pupils. The exercises are inspired by the work of a dedicated refugee teacher during the migrant influx in Greece. He used these three universal values in his work with displaced children. With connection - trust - compassion you can lay a firm foundation in yourself. These values can be used by everyone, in every school, for every child.

7.2 CONNECTION

"Vulnerability is the only bridge to connection". This quote highlights the core message of this chapter. Everyone is vulnerable but people often try to hide their vulnerability. As Brené Brown, research professor at the University of Houston, describes in her vulnerability paradox "it is the first thing I look in for you and the last thing I want you to see in me."

teachingrefugeechildren.com

https://twitter.com/brenebrown/status/354577580243951620?lang=en

Universal values in practice

You can only connect with someone else when you are connected to yourself. As you learn to know yourself (better) you will be make better contact with others. The other person is you. What gift does this child or colleague offer you? What can you learn about yourself and the other person through the connection? That is what this chapter is about.

1. Learn about your personal cultural history

personal cultural history

Everyone brings their own customs and traditions into a contact. We can be familiar with travel and watch National Geographic or Netflix documentaries about other cultures, but what about your knowledge of your own personal cultural history?

watch The DNA Journey

Feeling connected to your own history can give you strength, a sense of belonging, connection and self-assurance. Carrying out family tree research, talking with family members about family history or having your DNA profile analysed can give you a lot of insight and inspiration about your own identity. You can make surprising discoveries on this 'journey to your past and present'. In addition to being able to support your growth, feeling that we are all connected can also lead to the realisation that we all have more in common than we think. Just have a look at the movie The DNA Journey.

Weblink available at Sources at the end of this book.

2. Learn about the cultural history of your pupils

A. Make an inventory | If you have knowledge about the backgrounds of your pupils, children and their parents will feel this. They will pick up on your interest. This makes them feel a certain level of familiarity and safety with you. These are essential values for a warm pedagogical environment through which (traumatised) pupils can (again) open up to learning.

The following exercise will support you to feel more connected to the different cultures in your class. Based the list of names, make an inventory of the different countries of origin that are represented in your class. Do you know where Soumeya or Erasto were born and where their parents come from?

strengthen connection

Practical: Do you not teach or do you have multiple classes? Then choose 15 children that you are supporting or counselling.

Name of the child	**Culture(s) of origin**
1. _____	_____
2. _____	_____
3. _____	_____
4. _____	_____
5. _____	_____

Connecting Values, Multicultural Guidance for Primary Education
Hélène van Oudheusden

B. Increase your knowledge | 5 Tools for a better understanding of cultures

1. **Back to Syria**: the Dutch travel show host Floortje Dessing (Flora) visited Syria before the war. She returned to Syria in 2016 to get a clear picture of the war and to learn about experiences

Universal values in practice

of Syrian children. Her documentaries are available online with English and Arabic subtitles.
https://programma.bnnvara.nl/floortjeterugnaarsyrie/english
https://programma.bnnvara.nl/floortjeterugnaarsyrie/arab

2. **Google Earth**: view the geography and landmarks of countries via Google Earth.

3. **Power of symbols**: ask children and parents to bring symbols from their country of origin (rice, candle, photo etc.) and put them on a table in the classroom. A country can be devastated but the culture is held safe within the people themselves. Keeping in touch with this in the classroom increases feelings of safety and self-confidence in children. This can make them more open to learning.

self-confidence

4. **Flags all around**: hang up the national flag of each of the countries where the children have their roots. Do this in a way that indicates in which direction each county is. Obviously this is dependent on where you are teaching; in Europe you would place the flag of Eritrea on the south wall of the classroom, while the Afghani flag would be placed on the east wall and the flag of the country you are in in the middle of the ceiling. This tool supports the sense of one large community of different cultures in your group. If you ask the children and their parents to bring these symbols in themselves, you also stimulate parental involvement.

ancestors.unknown.org

5. **Ancestors Unknown** is an online educational program for primary and secondary age children. Children discover their own roots and those of other children in their class. This knowledge can lead to a better understanding of one's own roots and identity as well as compassion and solidarity with other children.

> **TIP** | *Are you a dean? A world map on the wall of your room always gives starting points for talks with newcomers.*

111

Extra tool
Netflix ''Daughters of Destiny' is a documentary about five girls from the lower caste in India ('the untouchables') who receive education to be able to provide for themselves and their families. See weblink at Inspirational reading and watching at the end of the book.

> *A country can be devastated but the culture is held safe within the people themselves.*

C. See what you do / will do differently | What are the benefits for you now that you know more about cultural similarities and differences? How does your improved knowledge alter your contact with the children in your class?

Name of the child	Culture(s) of origin	Effect of your new knowledge
1. _____	_____	_____
2. _____	_____	_____
3. _____	_____	_____
4. _____	_____	_____
5. _____	_____	_____

Connecting Values, Multicultural Guidance for Primary Education
Hélène van Oudheusden

> *It is easier to comfort a child when you have seen what he has been through.*

7.3 TRUST

Trust is a basic condition for successful education. This applies to the teacher's trust in themselves, trust between a child and their teacher, trust between the children, trust between the school's headmaster and the teacher, trust between a parent and a teacher. In the context of this chapter self-confidence is synonymous with trust - you start with self-confidence (trust in yourself) and with confidence (trust) in the other person.

A. Self-confident teacher?

An effective tool to measure your own self-confidence is the question: What is your added value for children? Everyone is 'replaceable' but it is also the case that you have unique qualities that make children happy to have you as their teacher. Which seven qualities combined (more is also okay!) make up your unique value to the school?

your unique value

1. Love for children

2. _____

3. _____

4. _____

5. _____

6. _____

7. _____

Curious what other teachers mentioned?
Persistence – sincere interest – self-reflection – willingness to communicate, even if things get difficult – finding practical solutions – love for children – humour – creativity

For inspiration: what would children, parents and colleagues miss if you did not work at school anymore?

3 Tools for more self-confidence
We gain self-confidence by trying and persisting. Waiting passively for self-confidence does not work...
1. Speak your mind in a meeting this week.
2. Stand up for yourself if an unpleasant situation with a colleague continues.
3. Start a new course or hobby with people you do not know yet.

self-confidence

B. (Self-)confident child?
Refugee children have often been through many experiences that test their faith in humanity. It requires patience and dedication from the teacher, the parents and the child themselves to rebuild this trust.

20-Year-old Rania from Syria filmed her flight from Kobane (Syria) to Austria (Europe). More than a million refugees made this journey in 2015/2016, sometimes alone, sometimes with family. For weblink to Rania's journey see Sources at the end of the book. The film gives insight into experiences that influence the (self-)confidence of refugee children. Which experiences can you name?

1. Hunger and exhaustion

2. _____

3. _____

Universal values in practice

C. We are the Best Country! - Trust exercise

Aim | Children learn to value each child's cultural talents and experiences, they can benefit from cooperation

Prepare | Plenty of A3 paper and colour markers in middle of a circle. Children sit in a circle. When working in nature please form a natural circle with wood for children to sit on – this promotes focus for children.

Your introduction | Raise your hand and let the fingers talk:
Index finger says I am always right because I am the first
Middle finger: I am the smartest because I am the tallest
Ring finger: I am the most beautiful because wedding bands go around me
Little finger says: I am the smallest one so I have to get my way

Within the circle children divide themselves over two, three, four or five groups, depending on the number of nationalities in class. For example one with African children, one with Arabic, one with European etc. On the A3 paper children write a Top 3 of why they are the best - being Syrian or African. Then you let wise Thumb speak: Oh my fingers/children what are you talking about…you have to cooperate with each other and with me otherwise the hand can't do anything. You need me to pick things up, to grasp something, to eat. Don't you see? We all have to work together to make things happen! How can you help others in your class or camp with your Top 3 of being the best? Talk with the children about how their Top 3 helps to promote the class or camp community. Do Syrian children think they are the smartest? Then they can improve the school system. Do African children think they are the strongest? Then they can train the Syrian children.

'Introduction with the hand' from UNHCR, The UN Refugee Agency. See weblink in the Sources. Refugee teacher Dionisis Pavlou has arranged the hand exercise to refer to countries in a camp or school.

3 Tools to stimulate (self-)confidence amongst refugee children

1. **Information** | If you know more or less what children have experienced they can feel (even) more at ease with you. You can get this information from the intake interview, from the news and from individual contact with children.
2. **Security** | A predictable daily structure offers children a sense of security and tranquillity. Starting and finishing your lessons on time provides them with a simple structure that will soon bear fruit.
3. **Mindfulness** | Mindfulness and concentration exercises are aimed at teaching with less stress and more harmony in class. Mindfulness can support (traumatised) children to feel at ease in their bodies (again). Always provide guidance from the care team or a professional specialised in trauma processing. See Part 8 Mindfulness for Refugee Children.

You'll find mindfulness exercises in Dutch, English and Arabic at YouTube Mindfulness in the Classroom.

7.4 COMPASSION

Compassion for yourself, for your vulnerability and persistence helps you to grow personally and professionally. You have probably come a long way to be able to teach like you do today. Crediting yourself for having gone through all you have experienced so far in life gives you grounding and an open view to what lies ahead of you.

compassion

It is often easier to feel compassion for others than for ourselves. But, if we do not compliment and support ourselves for what we (are trying to) do, we become dependent on other people's acknowledgement or praise. That is a bit of a pointless round trip: why not give it to yourself first? Then external acknowledgement will feel like a bonus. This is 'filling your own cup first' and gives you a strong self-care foundation.

A few self-reflection questions and suggestions to enhance compassion

What would you like to say to the 5-year-old version of yourself?
_____
_____

What can you do for someone today that you are having a fight with?
_____
_____

When you ask your body what it needs right now, what does it say?
_____
_____

If you are having trouble with unexpected behaviour from a young child remember that he was still in the womb only 5 or 6 years ago...
_____
_____

Put a rose in your class today to symbolise and share your compassion for yourself and the children. How did this influence your day?
_____
_____

Skip your lesson plan and ask the children what they would like to learn today. What were the results of this unexpected change in the school day?
_____
_____

Compassion for refugee children

Documentary 4.1 Miles by Daphne Matziaraki | The distance between Turkey and Lesvos (Greece) is 4.1 miles (6.6 km). This short film tells the story of a Greek coast guard captain who is suddenly faced with the rescue of refugees on the Aegean Sea between Europe and Turkey. The documentary is impressive and emotional and it will give you important background information on the plight of refugee children. For weblink please see Sources at the end of the book.

4.1 Miles

7.5 EXERCISES FOR TEACHERS ONLY

exercises for teachers

You can use the following exercises to prepare yourself to teach refugee children or to introduce your colleagues to this special vocation. These exercises give you the opportunity to strengthen the three core values (connection - trust – compassion) at school, through imagination and drama design. In most of the exercises the participants will empathise with the world of a refugee. Both on the journey as well as in the new homeland.

universal values

The exercises are suitable for school teams. These exercises are not suitable for performing with refugee children because they are likely to evoke painful emotional memories.

One Step Forward

Aim | Participants understand the plight of refugees

Prepare | 10 Role play cards with the following roles. One on each card.
- I am an unaccompanied minor, I arrived in your country this morning and I don't know where to go
- I am the manager of a refugee camp
- I am a doctor in a refugee camp for women and children

- I am a journalist writing an article on the refugee crisis
- I am teaching refugee children, part-time
- I am a refugee from Morocco, trying to get asylum in Europe
- I am a Rohingya refugee, I am volunteering in the camp and applying for asylum in France
- I am a single mother with four children in Colombia, I fled from Venezuela
- I am 8 years old and fled with my parents from Syria. I miss my dog, we couldn't take her with us on our journey

Make extra cards with other up-to-date roles relevant to your country.

Your introduction | Participants stand in a row, next to each other. Leave enough space in front of the participants for about 15 steps. The leader hands a card to each participant, the participants do not share the information on the card. The leader asks the participants to take one step forward if the following applies to the role on their card. If the statement does not apply the participant does not move.

- You have enough food and shelter
- You are able to go out at night, maybe to a theatre or to see a movie
- You are safe and warm
- You can travel freely
- You have enough money to cover your expenses
- You can practice your religion freely
- You can see a doctor when you need to
- You are insured for health care
- You have access to a library

The leader asks the participants to share what role they played. How does it feel to be a doctor or a refugee? What (human) rights do you miss as a refugee? Was the 'refugee' only able to take one step forward? Invite participants to express their thoughts and emotions.

Come to one or several conclusions and close the exercise by thanking all of the participants. Ask the participants to visualise that they are themselves again (not playing a role anymore - it is important not to carry the emotions of the role with them the rest of the day. Take the cards back or leave them with the participants as a reminder of this exercise

UNHCR, The UN Refugee Agency. For weblink see Sources at the end of the book.

The Web of All Together

Aim | Experience feeling connected with everyone

Prepare | A ball of wool

Your introduction | Participants make a circle. The leader tosses the ball of wool to a participant while holding onto the end of the thread. He calls out the name of the participant and expresses what he wishes for the participant. Each participant does the same for other participants in the circle, holding onto the thread every time.

This exercise creates a web of good wishes, warm welcome and connectednes. At the end the web is placed carefully on the floor. Have someone take a photo or make a drawing about the web to help continue this feeling of all being together throughout the school year.

TIP | *Teaching resources in several languages to learn about the plight of refugee children can also be found on: http://www.unhcr.org/teaching-resources.html*

Universal values in practice

7.6 DO'S FOR SCHOOL DIRECTORS

To enable the previous suggestions for teaching refugee children, school leaders should take the following into account:

school leaders

1. **Put self-care for your team members on the agenda** at every meeting. Teachers who are aware that there is sufficient emphasis on their well-being will pay more attention to their boundaries and possibilities and are less likely to suffer burnout.
2. **Train your colleagues in multicultural competencies.** Introspection on teaching children from other cultures is the starting point. Please see the questions on self-reflection for teachers in Chapter 1.4.

    introspection: see also Chapter 1.4

3. **Ensure that teachers are up-to-date with international news:** do they know about the EU-Turkey agreement regarding refugees? Are they watching or reading the news regularly? Interest in (and knowledge about) the background of their pupils benefits the quality of their teaching.
4. **Provide (or participate in) an inspiring network** with fellow school managers in the area. This supports self-care and enables you to introduce new ideas at school after consulting with colleagues.

    networking

5. **Watch the video 'The DNA Journey' with your team.** We have more in common than we think and this video says it all. For weblink see Inspirational reading and watching at the end of the book.

NOTES

PART 8

Mindfulness for Refugee Children

"The most precious gift we can offer others is our presence. When mindfulness embraces those we love, they will bloom like flowers."

Thich Nhat Hanh

With gratitude to Jon Kabat-Zinn (founder of modern mindfulness), Zen Master Thich Nhat Hanh and His Holiness the 14th Dalai Lama (Educating the heart) for bringing us mindfulness.

TAGS

automatic pilot – conscious pilot | breathe! | one – five - ten minute(s) mindfulness | mindful listening | mindful speech | metta meditation

8 | MINDFULNESS FOR REFUGEE CHILDREN

YOUTUBE | On Mindfulness in the Classroom you will find 'Bodycheck' and 'Listen to the Sounds' in English, Arabic and Greek.

8.1 INTRODUCTION

There is a rise in the use of mindfulness or attention training classes in schools for refugee children. Mindfulness can help children to regain confidence in their bodies and minds again. See also Chapter 3.5.

facebook.com/thichnhathanh

The effects of mindfulness are constantly being researched by universities. Research shows, amongst other things, that mindfulness can help teachers and pupils to deal with feelings of stress better. The atmosphere in the classroom often improves during and after attention training. As mindfulness trainer I have noticed that mindfulness is also suitable for children with symptoms of AD(H)D and Autism.

By using mindfulness, both the teacher and the children learn to view their thoughts and emotions from a distance. You start by recognising your 'automatic pilot' - your unconscious, fixed reactions to impulses. By becoming aware of these you create (short) moments of rest between impulse and action. You can then gradually transform the 'automatic pilot' into the 'conscious pilot'. Think first, then act.

invite your other pilot

Think first, act second examples:
- Are WhatsApp messages controlling me or do I determine if and when I respond?

- Do I choose to start studying at the last moment or do I take good care of myself by allowing more preparation time?
- Is it wise to respond directly to what someone else asks me or should I take some time to investigate what feels good to me?

With mindfulness teacher and child discover how they can 'reset' themselves if they have difficulties focussing. See weblink Mindful Schools at Sources for information about research on mindfulness.

advantages

8.2 ADVANTAGES OF MINDFULNESS FOR TEACHERS AND CHILDREN

- Better focus and concentration
- Increased self-awareness
- Less stress for children and teachers
- Stronger school climate
- Less stress around tests
- Better impulse control and a decrease in violence
- Increased problem solving capacity in conflicts
- Increased rest
- Appropriate responses to challenging emotions
- Growth of empathy and understanding of others

Mindful Schools – Integrating Mindfulness into Education

8.3 WHEN DO YOU USE MINDFULNESS EXERCISES?

- For yourself as a teacher when you start your day
- As a starting point when you sit in a circle with your class at the start of the school day
- In case of unrest in the classroom
- Prior to a test or exam

- As a brief time-out between lessons
- Before or during important conversations (with parents, children, colleagues or supervisors)

8.4 BREATHE IN, BREATHE OUT

By focussing on your breathing you are directly in the here and now. When you are anxious or scared your breathing might become shallow and high in your chest. Breathing exercises will help you to deepen your breathing and to become calmer. Children love to hear you explain that their breathing is their best friend. It can be their point of focus to feel calm again. Our breath is always with us and helps us to discover and monitor how we feel. simple but powerful breathing exercise is to place your hand on your belly and to breathe in and out 10 times, feeling your belly move towards your hand. How do you feel afterwards?

breathe!

For the teacher You can place your hand on your belly without other people noticing. That makes this exercise practical to use during talks or meetings where you want to slow down or give yourself new energy.

For the children Focussing on their breath when they feel stress, helps them to become more relaxed. When quarrelling with a class mate it helps to take 3 deep breaths before reacting. This is a time out that helps change the automatic pilot ('You hurt me so I will hit you.') into the conscious pilot ('I am hurt, how can I respond to this?').

invite your other pilot

8.5 ONE MINUTE MINDFULNESS

1. Listen to the silence around you for one minute.
2. Imagine you have come from Mars and have never seen a pen before. Look at your pen for one minute.

one minute mindfulness

3. Feel how firmly your feet rest on the floor, for one minute.
4. Smile to yourself for one minute.
5. Smile at your neighbour for one minute.
6. Walk in silence through the corridor for one minute.
7. Run for one minute.
8. Taste your drink consciously for one minute.
9. Have children look at nice picture on the board for one minute. Remove or cover the picture and ask them to draw it.
10. Count how often you exhale in one minute.

five to ten minutes mindfulness

8.6 FIVE TO TEN MINUTES MINDFULNESS

Listen to the Sounds

YOUTUBE | Mindfulness in the Classroom – Listen to the Sounds
Hélène van Oudheusden   English – Arabic – Greek - Dutch

Let the children relax on the floor or in their chairs. Ask them to close their eyes and concentrate for 30 seconds on the sounds outside the classroom, then on the sounds inside the classroom and finally on the sounds inside their bodies. Afterwards, let them come back quietly and discuss what everyone heard. Didn't everyone hear the same sounds? That is fine, everybody focuses slightly differently. All answers are okay.

> **TIP |** *Busy children? Do the exercise from outside inwards. Passivity or low-energy in class? Try the exercise from inwards outwards to help children open up to the outside world.*

Raisin exercise

YOUTUBE | Mindfulness in de Klas – Krentoefening

Hélène van Oudheusden   in Dutch only

Prepare |
- Raisins and worksheets. Instead of raisins you can also use fruit or chocolate.
- The GoZen cartoon 'Mindful Eating' (with chocolate) will give children an impression of the exercise.
See weblink at Sources.

Your introduction | During this attention exercise you experience the five senses. The senses are seeing, feeling, hearing, smelling and tasting. Noticing and using your senses can help you to focus or concentrate better in the classroom or at home. For example, look at your pen for 5 seconds as if you have never seen a pen before.

Pause for 5 seconds

You may notice that you are feeling a bit calmer now. If you regularly do this kind of focusing exercise, you will feel more relaxed and your school work will probably be easier. The raisin exercise is done with curiosity. Pretend you have never seen a raisin before in your life.

power of Zen

> **TIPS FOR YOUR PUPILS |**
> - *'If your mind wanders during the exercise, try to bring your attention back to your breathing.'*
> - *'Make sure that your classmates can do the exercise, try not to disturb each other. If you cannot keep up with the exercise, then just sit quietly. Time will pass and next we will do something that you will enjoy.'*

Sit quietly and relax in your chair. You can close your eyes or – if you do not want to – then look at the table instead. Breathe in and out a few times without making a sound. Feel how firmly you are sitting and try to keep your shoulders low. Imagine yourself in your favourite place.

1. If you had your eyes closed, open them and look at the raisin on your table. Admire it as if it is the first time you have ever seen a raisin... what does it look like? What do you notice? Which colours do you see in the raisin? Do you see the shadow of the raisin on the table?
2. Carefully pick it up and place it in your hand. Rub your finger gently over the raisin and feel its skin. Feel the ridges and unevenness. Is the raisin is soft or hard? Is it smooth on the outside or rough?
3. Then bring the raisin close to your ear with two fingers. Gently squeeze it but don't squash it. What do you hear?
4. Next, put the raisin between your lips, in front of your teeth. Feel the structure and try to keep it there for as long as possible. If you are distracted by thoughts, try to focus on your breathing again.
5. Now put the raisin in your mouth but do not chew it. Put it under your tongue and leave it there for a while. You may want to chew, but do not do that yet. Let the thought of chewing fly away like a cloud and focus on the raisin.
6. Finally, chew the raisin slowly once or twice and taste the flavour. What do you taste? Is it the taste you expected or do you notice something new? Swallow the raisin and enjoy the lingering taste for a while.

TIP | *Try to eat the first bite of your lunch just like the raisin exercise. Does your lunch taste different?*

TIP | *By making a drawing of the raisin children can concentrate even better.*

WORKSHEET

Fill in what you noticed during the different parts of this exercise on the worksheet while keeping your focus on yourself.

Your experiences:

I see_____

I feel _____

I hear_____

I smell_____

I taste_____

Make a drawing of your raisin here.

Body check

YOUTUBE | Mindfulness in the Classroom – Bodycheck

Hélène van Oudheusden   English – Arabic – Greek - Dutch

Sit or lay down, relax and be aware of your body on your chair or on the mattress. When you do the body check you just observe, you do not follow your thoughts or emotions. Breathe quietly and feel every part of your body.

1. Breathe in through your nose and out through your mouth.
2. Imagine that you are under a shower that is washing away all of your thoughts, emotions and feelings of stress, let them go down the drain.
3. Imagine that you are in a pleasant place.
4. Feel your feet on the ground, feel your toes, nails, the tops and bottoms of your feet, the heels and ankles.
5. Continue to your lower legs, knees, thighs and your pelvic area, all the way up to your belly, stomach, heart area and shoulders.
6. Feel your arms: upper arms, elbows, forearms, wrists, hands, fingers and the tips of your nails.
7. Feel your throat and neck then up to your head (front, sides and back) right up to the crown.
8. From the crown of your head work back down in the same way until you reach your feet again.

> *Just observe, don't dwell on your thoughts and feelings while doing the body check.*

Metta Meditation

metta meditation

Metta (loving-kindness meditation) supports you to cultivate loving compassion and kindness for yourself and for all creatures (from Buddhism). Feel loving compassion for yourself in all parts/cells of your body. Then say to yourself:

I wish you to be happy
I wish you to be free and without worry
I wish you to be healthy
I wish you to be safe

Then imagine saying the same words to someone you love, to someone you are neutral towards and to someone you find it difficult to relate to.

Have children do the metta meditation once a week with classmates in mind and see how this exercise changes the atmosphere in your class.

Mindful Listening

Put the children into pairs, sitting opposite each other. Each child can talk for one minute about, for example, the weekend, the break, an exciting test or any other subject. The other child listens and says only 'I understand you' or nods in agreement. The purpose of this exercise is to allow children to practice listening without responding or giving advice. Then they change roles and repeat the experience.

mindful listening

Mindful Speech

Find a quiet time when you can sit down and read the following sentences aloud to yourself. As you read, follow the instructions that the text provides. Each asterisk indicates that you should pause and count to three.

mindful speech

> *To learn to speak mindfully is to learn to consider what I am about to say even before I say it.*
> *
> *When I speak mindfully, I place a pause before each sentence.*
> *
> *This pause gives me time to make important choices.*

*

I will decide the content of what I am about to say.

*

I will decide the tone of my words.

*

I will choose how calmly and clearly I say my words.

*

As I read these sentences, I will place a pause at the end of each one.

*

This pause will last several seconds.

*

I will listen carefully to the sound of that pause and the silence it creates.

*

At first, for practice, I will count to three during each pause.

*

This practice will promote the act of pausing after each sentence.

*

The slight pause I insert after each sentence gives me the opportunity to consider and mindfully evaluate the content of my next thought.

*

When I am mindless - when I live the habit driven life - I tend to string all my thoughts together without a mindful pause for evaluation.

*

This fosters thoughtless speech based on emotion, prejudice and impulse rather than careful, deliberate speaking.

*

My mindless speech is reactive; my mindful speech is purposeful and calm.

*

The truth of mindful speech rings through like a clear bell.

*

This is because the slight pause I place between my sentences allows me to determine if what I'm about to say is truth or opinion, is helpful or harmful, is praise or is criticism.

*

That small pause, in fact, gives me a universe of choices that I never knew were available to me before.

*

With that pause, I can control my angry voice and I can find better words of kindness or compassion.

*

I will remember this exercise, and the next time I speak I will know to insert a pause before each sentence - a pause so small that those who hear me will not be able to tell. But I will know that I have inserted mindfulness into my speech.

Frederik Burggraf

Relaxation exercise with coloured crayons

1. Ask your pupils to put their crayon box on the table.
2. Have them take all of the crayons out of the box without talking.
3. Ask them to put the crayons back into the box again.
4. If you wish, let them repeat this exercise.

Afterwards you can ask the children what they experienced during the exercise. What did they feel? Did they have certain thoughts? Did they have an opinion about the exercise? All answers are okay. If a child says they didn't like the exercise, just say 'thank you for sharing'. This allows children to experience that all feelings matter. That is the core of mindfulness: observing what is happening inside yourself without judgment.

Grounding exercise 'Strong like a Tree'

Put your feet firmly on the floor ('stick them to the floor')
bend your knees slightly
put your hand on your stomach
inhale a few times through your nose or mouth
your legs are the tree trunk, your arms the branches
move when you imagine feeling the rain, wind and the sunshine

Focus on how firmly your feet are on the floor
bend your knees slightly
rub your arms and your legs
shake your arms and legs
you are completely relaxed!

> **TEACHER TIP** | *If you stand 'Strong like a Tree' in the classroom you will feel more empowered. You can experience a clear overview of what can and what needs to be done during the day. Ask children if you are allowed to touch their shoulder briefly before and after the exercise. You can feel a difference in their body strength. Are they standing strong and do they simultaneously move their arms (lightly)? Explain the connection between their posture and (emotional) situations in life. If you move with a situation, you are able to grow your resilience. For example: reeds bend with the wind and lay down almost flat in a violent storm but are able to spring back up unbroken.*

Blow your thoughts into the balloon

Teacher preparation: enough balloons for each child and for yourself
Let the children relax on the floor or in their seats. Ask them to close their eyes and concentrate on a thought that disturbs them. Invite them to blow up the balloon. With every breath they blow the

worrying thoughts into the balloon. The children thank themselves and the balloon. Ask them to fill the space where the worry was (their heart? belly? head?) with fresh, gold coloured energy. How do they feel afterwards? Take the balloons away at the end of the day so the worries have left the classroom.

8.7 TEN MINUTES MINDFULNESS

ten minutes mindfulness

Body check with movement

YOUTUBE | Mindfulness in the Classroom – Bodycheck

Hélène van Oudheusden   English – Arabic – Greek - Dutch

Sit or lay down, relax and be aware of your body on your chair or on the mattress. When you do the body check with movement you just observe, you do not follow your thoughts or emotions. Breathe quietly and feel every part of your body.

1. Breathe in through your nose and out through your mouth.
2. Imagine that you are under a shower that is washing away all of your thoughts, emotions and feelings of stress, let them go down the drain.
3. Imagine that you are in a pleasant place.
4. Slowly move your feet on the ground, feel your toes, nails, the top and bottom of the feet, move the heels and ankles.
5. Continue to gently move your lower legs, knees, thighs and your pelvic area, move your upper body all the way up to your shoulders.
6. Stretch your arms: upper arms, elbows, forearms, wrists, hands and your finger tips.
7. Move your neck and your head (front, sides and back) right up to your crown.
8. From the crown of your head work back down in the same way until you reach your feet again.

Just observe, don't dwell on your thoughts and feelings while doing the body check with movement.

> **SUGGESTION** | *Making movements in an anticlockwise direction (to the left) helps you to unwind, moving in a clockwise direction supports you to recharge yourself with new, fresh energy.*

Mindful Walking

forest bathing:
www.shinrin-yoku.org

Go to a park or playing field where the children can walk in silence. Ask them to focus on the soles of their feet while walking. Every time they get lost in thought invite them to take their attention back to their breathing. Give varying instructions during walk with them:

- Focus on the colour red in nature
- Listen to the birds
- Feel the warmth of the sun (or the chill of the wind)

Cloud Gazing

Outside: the children lay on their backs on grass. They look at the movements of the clouds. Clouds come and go like thoughts. This is an easy way to explain children that you don't have to follow/act on every thought. They just come and go and in the meantime you can observe and think about your best response.

Disclaimer: we have tried to credit the sources of all the exercises included in this book. Anyone thinking they are the creator of an exercise not credited to them should please contact us via info@helenevanoudheusden.nl.

INSPIRATIONAL READING AND WATCHING

On www.teachingrefugeechildren.com you will find all links in the book. Clicking the links makes it easier for you to reach background information.

teachingrefugeechildren.com

Ancestors Unknown
http://www.ancestors-unknown.org

Books and articles for teachers
Verbindende waarden, multiculturele begeleiding in het basisonderwijs, Hélène van Oudheusden, www.verbindendewaarden.nl, only available in Dutch.

Aesop's Fables, www.taleswithmorals.com

Fast Growing Seeds for Kids
www.craftulate.com/fast-growing-seeds-kids

Forest Bathing
www.shinrin-yoku.org

Refugee Children in the Classroom, Hélène van Oudheusden, April 2016, PO Management, www.teachingrefugeechildren.com

Teaching Resources, UNHCR (in several languages)
www.unhcr.org/teaching-resources.html

Inspirational reading and watching

Books for refugee children
Is the school budget limited? Look for second hand books on Amazon, eBay and Bol.com.

Lost and Found Cat: The True Story of Kunkush's Incredible Journey by Doug Kuntz, Amy Shrodes, Sue Cornelison

Travelling Tales by various authors

Four Feet, Two Sandals by Karen Lynn Williams

Alfie: (The Turtle That Disappeared) by Thyra Heder

Educational activities in nature for children of refugees and locals
Mikros Dounias (Lesvos, Greece)
http://en.mikrosdounias.eu

Google Earth
www.google.com/earth

Mindfulness in the Classroom
YOUTUBE | Mindfulness in the Classroom - Hélène van Oudheusden
Mindfulness exercises in English, Arabic, Greek and Dutch
www.youtube.com

YOUTUBE | GoZen Mindful Eating (with chocolate)

Movies
4.1 Miles by Daphne Matziaraki
www.nytimes.com/video

Back to Syria, Floortje Dessing, BNNVARA
https://programma.bnnvara.nl/floortjeterugnaarsyrie/english
https://programma.bnnvara.nl/floortjeterugnaarsyrie/arab

Quote from Dutch Speech Therapy Association (www.nvlf.nl) is from 'De kinderen van juf Kiet' by Petra Lataster-Czisch and Peter Lataster
www.dekinderenvanjufkiet.nl

Daughters of Destiny, Netflix
www.netflix.com

Music in the classroom
Classical Mondscheinsonate, W.A. Beethoven or Clair de Lune,
C. Debussy
http://www.youtube.com/watch?v=-LXl4y6D-QI

Search online for: Arabic – African - Indian relaxing music or Relaxing anti-stress music (some videos include beautiful pictures for meditation)

On foreign education systems
Nuffic, The Dutch organisation for internationalisation in education
www.nuffic.nl/en/subjects

Refugee children and resilience; Empowerment, participation and subjective wellbeing
Siv Førde
https://brage.bibsys.no/xmlui/bitstream/id/114221/SivForde07.pdf.

Tool-kit for teachers
UNHCR Teaching about refugees, Guidance on working with refugee children struggling with stress and trauma http://www.unhcr.org/publications/education/59d346de4/teaching-refugees-guidance-working-refugee-children-struggling-stress-trauma.html

SOURCES

Brown, B., Daring Greatly. Amsterdam, A.W. Bruna Uitgevers B.V., 2017

Brown, B., The Gifts of Imperfection. Amsterdam, A.W. Bruna Uitgevers B.V., 2017

Brown, B., Quote: "The vulnerability paradox: It's the first thing I look for in you and the last thing I want you to see in me. #Connection"
https://twitter.com/brenebrown/status/354577580243951620?lang=en

Burggraf, F., Mindful Speech
http://www.dayonepublishing.com/VMC/Exercises/MindfulSpeech.html

Campbell, J., The Hero's Journey Copyright © 1990, 2003 Joseph Campbell Foundation, p. 217; Copyright © 2014 Joseph Campbell Foundation, p. 253

Child Migrants (Migration Data Portal)
https://migrationdataportal.org/search?text=child%20migrants&theme=&tags=&category=

Connecting Learning with Emotions by Harry O'Malley
From: https://www.edutopia.org/article/connecting-learning-emotions

Coppens, L., Schneijderberg, M., van Kregten, C., Lesgeven aan getraumatiseerde kinderen. Amsterdam, B.V. Uitgeverij SWP, 2016

Escape from Syria: Rania's Odyssey video
https://www.youtube.com/watch?v=EDHwt-ooAi4

EU-Turkey Statement & Action Plan
http://www.europarl.europa.eu/portal/en

Eurostat
http://ec.europa.eu/eurostat/web/asylum-and-managed-migration/data/database

Gibran, K., The Prophet. England, Oneworld Publications, 1999

Grant Rankin, Ph.D.,J., The Teacher Burnout Epidemic, Part 1 of 2, 22 November 2016
From: https://www.psychologytoday.com/us/blog/much-more-common-core/201611/the-teacher-burnout-epidemic-part-1-2

'Introduction with the hand' from UNHCR, The UN Refugee Agency, Συμβίωση: Σχέδιο Δράσης για την προώθηση της ανεκτικότητας και την πρόληψη του ρατσισμού στο σχολείο (page 43-45). The Right Start, Amnesty International within the framework of initiative LIFT OFF.

Mind Tools Content Team, Forming, Storming, Norming, and Performing, Understanding the Stages of Team Formation. No date of publishing on website
From: https://www.mindtools.com/pages/article/newLDR_86.htm

Mindful Schools
www.mindfulschools.org

'One Step Forward' from UNHCR, The UN Refugee Agency, Συμβίωση: Σχέδιο Δράσης για την προώθηση της ανεκτικότητας και την πρόληψη του ρατσισμού στο σχολείο (page 46-52). Compasito, European Council

Research on Mindfulness via Mindful Schools
https://www.mindfulschools.org/about-mindfulness/research/

Reshaping the Trauma of Refugee Children in in Lesvos, Doctors without Borders, National Geographic
https://www.youtube.com/watch?v=V6IVZ569wsk

Somé, M.P., Ritual: Power, Healing and Community. Copyright © Swan Raven & Company, 1997

Statistics Netherlands, CBS en TNO: Een op de zeven werknemers heeft burn-outklachten, 16 November 2015
From: https://www.cbs.nl

The DNA Journey by Momondo
https://www.youtube.com/watch?v=tyaEQEmt5ls

The Dublin Regulation
http://www.unhcr.org/4a9d13d59.pdf

Thich Nhat Hanh, Quote: "The most precious gift we can offer others is our presence. When mindfulness embraces those we love, they will bloom like flowers." https://plumvillage.org/ and Facebook.com/ThichNhatHanh

UNHCR, The UN Refugee Agency, Mialy Dermish and others, Teaching About Refugees, Guidance on working with refugee children struggling with stress and trauma, 2017
From: http://www.unhcr.org/59d346de4

UNHCR, Figures at a Glance
From: http://www.unhcr.org/figures-at-a-glance.html

(in Greek) UNHCR, The UN Refugee Agency, Συμβίωση: Σχέδιο Δράσης για την προώθηση της ανεκτικότητας και την πρόληψη του ρατσισμού στο σχολείο.
From: http://collections.internetmemory.org/unhcr/20171002021437/http://www.unhcr.gr/fileadmin/Greece/Extras/education_symbiosis/Symbiosis_project_manual_final.pdf

United Nations, Convention on the Rights of the Child
https://www.ohchr.org/EN/ProfessionalInterest/Pages/CRC.aspx or Google for YouTube videos on this subject

Van Oudheusden, H., Refugee children in the classroom, On 250.000 children travelling Europe on their way to a brighter future, PO Management, April 2016 (in Dutch).
See for official English translation: https://www.teachingrefugeechildren.com/

Vostanis, P., How to help refugee children get through the trauma of what's happened to them, 25 August 2016.
From: https://theconversation.com/how-to-help-refugee-children-get-through-the-trauma-of-whats-happened-to-them-64335

http://www.vocativ.com/news/230358/wont-someone-think-of-the-children/index.html

EXTRA FOR READERS

For Teaching Refugee Children Seminars and for more educational materials please visit www.teachingrefugeechildren.com.

Use your login code to view the links in the book on www.teachingrefugeechildren.com.

Your login code: TRC

www.ingramcontent.com/pod-product-compliance
Lightning Source LLC
Chambersburg PA
CBHW080452170426
43196CB00016B/2775